Books are to be returned on or before the last date below.

LIVERPOOL EVERYMAN AND PLAYHOUSE

"Liverpool Playhouse and Everyman theatres are currently enjoying a fresh lease of life"

Independent on Sunday

Since January 2004, Liverpool Everyman and Playhouse have become full-time producing theatres once again, with a programme of homegrown work which alternates between the two venues, so that there is a continuous presence of theatre 'Made in Liverpool'.

Our aim is for these theatres to be firmly rooted in their community, yet both national and international in their cultural scope, offering audiences a rich and varied theatrical diet and putting Liverpool's theatre firmly back on the map. Recent, highly acclaimed productions have included Corin Redgrave in *The Entertainer*; Adrian Mitchell's adaptation of *The Mayor of Zalamea*; a co-production with Oxford Stage Company of Behan's *The Quare Fellow*; a rare double-bill of Noël Coward one-act plays, the European première of Dael Orlandersmith's Pulitzer-nominated play, *Yellowman* (which transferred to Hampstead Theatre); August Wilson's jazz-age drama *Ma Rainey's Black Bottom* and, in June, the world première of *Fly*, Katie Douglas's debut play.

Now, with *The Kindness of Strangers* and *Urban Legend* as the core of the Everyman's 40th birthday season, new plays and new writers are taking their rightful place at the heart of our programme. This theatre is at its best when it is a creative launchpad, and this intimate space provides a very special environment in which to experience a theatrical beginning.

This is an extremely dynamic period for the Everyman and Playhouse, with a major expansion in production, a passionate commitment to new writing, and a rapidly growing community programme. We believe that this expansion is the only appropriate response to the needs of the communities of Merseyside, to the great reservoir of local talent, and to the creative challenge of Liverpool's Capital of Culture status in 2008.

Gemma Bodinetz
Artistic Director

Deborah Aydon
Executive Director

For further information about our programme, please call 0151 709 4776, or see www.everymanplayhouse.com

LIFE BEGINS

Forty years ago a great theatrical tradition began in a crumbling ex-chapel on the corner of Hope Street.
The Everyman was born on 28th September 1964, and quickly built a reputation for ground-breaking work. A succession of visionary directors, exciting writers, and bold acting companies kept the flame alive for decades, and the Everyman has been the crucible for an astonishing range of theatrical talent. This dynamic space has generated a prodigious range of shows, from new writing to reinvented classics, from music theatre to political drama, from the mad and the mischievous to the seriously seminal. Always ambitious, never predictable, the Everyman is a Liverpool original.

We feel the most fitting way to celebrate the Everyman's tradition of reinvention is by focussing on the future, with two world premières of new Liverpool plays, Tony Green's *The Kindness of Strangers* and Laurence Wilson's *Urban Legend.* These theatres are now passionately committed to supporting new writing, and we have a wide range of activities geared towards developing the plays and the playwrights of the future. If you would like more information on new writing at the Everyman and Playhouse – either as an aspiring playwright or as an audience member with a passion for the new – please contact our Literary Department on 0151 708 3700 or at literary@everymanplayhouse.com

Around these two premières we have sprinkled a range of other events which celebrate the Everyman's history, bring some great stalwarts back into the fold, and bring home some Liverpool plays that have enjoyed success elsewhere but not yet been seen in this city. And alongside the celebrations, we have set up the Life Begins Fund which will enable us to commission two new writers each year in the lead-up to Liverpool's Capital of Culture year 2008. The Life Begins lead funders are the Granada Foundation and the PH Holt Charitable Trust, and if you would like to support the Fund, please contact our Development Department on 0151 706 9115.

CRITICAL RESPONSE TO OUR RECENT PRODUCTIONS AT THE EVERYMAN

KEVIN HARVEY AND CECILIA NOBLE IN *YELLOWMAN*

YELLOWMAN

"***** *Powerfully engaging*"
THE INDEPENDENT

"*Cecilia Noble and Kevin Harvey's dazzling performances are compassionate, intelligent and tough... Brighter than that Southern sunshine*"
THE TIMES

EVE DALLAS, DAVID JENKINS AND SIMON DONALDSON IN *FLY*

FLY

"*If the quality of Fly is anything to go by, the Everyman's future looks bright.*"
DAILY POST

"*Katie Douglas's debut play… hooks the emotional heart of a situation and reels it in with dialogue as taut as a straining fishing line. ****"*
THE GUARDIAN

TOM GEORGESON AND MARK THEODORE IN *THE KINDNESS OF STRANGERS*

THE KINDNESS OF STRANGERS

"**** *The Everyman could wish for no finer 40th anniversary present than a return to form.*"
THE GUARDIAN

Photography by Christian Smith

Also at the Playhouse...

The Entertainer

"***** *Very moving indeed*"
THE TIMES

The Astonished Heart and Still Life

"*Expertly acted (and) beautifully designed*"
THE DAILY TELEGRAPH

Ma Rainey's Black Bottom

"*Gemma Bodinetz's evocative, handsomely acted revival ****"*
THE GUARDIAN

CREDITS

THE CAST (IN ALPHABETICAL ORDER)

Wayne	Mark Arends
Bobbo	Paul Duckworth
Horse	Al T Kossy
Robbie	Nick Moss

THE COMPANY

Writer	Laurence Wilson
Director	Dawn Walton
Designer	Soutra Gilmour
Lighting Designer	Natasha Chivers
Sound Designer	Sean Pritchard
Costume Supervisor	Marie Jones
Casting Director	Julia Horan
Dramaturg	Suzanne Bell
Company Stage Manager	Jamie Byron
Deputy Stage Manager	Pin Dix
Assistant Stage Manager	Jo Heffernan
Lighting Operator	Marc Williams/ Lindsey Bell
Sound Operator	Sean Pritchard/ Mary Cummings
Set Construction	Liverpool Everyman and Playhouse workshop/ Liverpool Scenic workshop
Cover Image	Jon Barraclough

With thanks to: Sam Kent, Jason Mcquaide, Mike Gray and John Traynor.

Urban Legend was commissioned by Liverpool Everyman and Playhouse and received its world première at Everyman Theatre, Liverpool, on 29 October 2004.

CAST

MARK ARENDS WAYNE

Mark trained at LAMDA graduating in July 2003.

Mark's theatre credits include:
Fierce: An Urban Myth (The Traverse and The Assembly Rooms, Edinburgh); *Dealing* (Etcetera, London) and *Tamburlaine the Great* (The Rose, London).

Television includes: *Hollyoaks*.

Film includes: *Pride and Prejudice*.

Mark has also made a short film for the National Film and Television School and taken part in workshops for the young writers project at the Royal Court.

PAUL DUCKWORTH BOBBO

Paul's theatre credits include:
Golden Boy, *Man Who Stole a Winter Coat* and *The Corrupted Angel* (National tours with Base Chorus Company, including the Royal Opera House); *Slappers and Slapheads* (Royal Court and Empire Theatres, Liverpool and the Opera House, Manchester); *River Fever* (Unity Theatre); *Moving Voices* (Sheffield Crucible); *The Man who Cracked* (National Tour with Spike Theatre Company) and most recently, Robert Farquar's *You are Here* (Unity Theatre).

Television includes: *Brookside* and *Courtroom*.

Film includes: *Backbeat*.

CAST

AL T KOSSY HORSE

Al is one of Liverpool's best known and best loved character actors, whose roots are in musical hall, where he worked for many years.

Al's theatre credits include:
Macbeth, The Ale House, The Sunshine Boys, Talent, All in Good Time, Twopence to Cross the Mersey, Surf's Up and many Pantomimes.

Television credits include: *Grange Hill, Brookside, Linda Green, Eyes Down, Cops, The Lakes, Hillsborough, Springhill, Jake's Progress, Rich Deceiver, Cracker, Blood on the Dole, Watchdog* and *The Man From The Pru.*

Radio credits include: *Kossy Korner* and *Merseysiders.*

Al was a highly acclaimed stand-up comedian and impressionist who toured the world including America where he received the American Army Theatre Award for working with such stars as Sammy Davis Jnr, Brook Benton, Jane Mansfield and many more.

NICK MOSS ROBBIE

Nick's first experiences of the Everyman were during his years with the Everyman Youth theatre. Previous professional work at the Everyman includes *The Mayor Of Zalamea* and *Scouse.*

Nick's theatre credits include:
The People are Friendly, Made of Stone and *Naturalised* (Royal Court, London); *Huddersfield, Coming Around Again* and *Enjoy* (West Yorkshire Playhouse) and *An Evening With Gary Lineker* (Oldham Coliseum).

Television includes: *The Bill, Casualty, Paradise Heights, Smack the Pony, Merseybeat, Doctors, Always and Everyone, Liverpool One, Lifeforce, Heart Beat, City Central, Cops, Retrace, Hillsborough, Police 2020* and *Emmerdale.*

Film includes: *Trauma, The Calcium Kid, Mean Machine, Al's Lads, Going Off Big Time* and *Heart.*

COMPANY

LAURENCE WILSON WRITER

Liverpool has been Laurence's home and inspiration since he was four. Laurence is a member of Liverpool Everyman and Playhouse Associates. He was one of the three original members of the Liverpool Everyman and Playhouse's pilot Writers' Attachment Scheme 2002-3 during which time *Urban Legend* received a successful reading at Soho House Theatre in London. Laurence has played many roles as an actor and was also a singer-songwriter, before turning to writing.

His previous stage work includes: *Surf's Up* (Unity Theatre, Liverpool, The Vampire Lounge and Contact Theatre, Manchester); *Crash Test Dummies* (with Liverpool Lunchtime Theatre); *Mezz'ed Up* (Unity Theatre); Co-adaptor of *Dick Whittington* (Neptune theatre, Liverpool and Theatre Royal, St Helens) and *Journey to Mars* (a young person's play, produced at Skelmersdale High).

Work for television includes: *Drug Runners* (for Conker Media, Mersey TV); the short films *Buckets* (Channel 4) and *Card for the Clubs* (in development with Conker Media, Mersey TV).

Plays for radio include: *Dark Tayle*.

Laurence was nominated for the Best New Talent in Theatre for the Liverpool Echo Awards in 2002 and for Two Manchester Evening News Awards: Best New Play and Best Fringe Production in 2003 for *Surf's Up* at the Contact. He is also currently developing a children's cartoon called *Dangerous Clowns* and a television series called *Mythic Heights*.

DAWN WALTON DIRECTOR

Dawn's recent work includes: *Big Voices* (RSC); *Winners* (Young Vic); *Serjeant Musgrave's Dance* and *Balm In Gilead* (Corbett Theatre); *Glow* (Theatre Centre); *The Changeling* (Mamamissi Productions); *Rampage, Workers Writes, Drag-On* and *The Shining* (Royal Court); *The Blacks* (Young Vic Studio); *Strings* (Clean Break TC); *Of Mice and Men* (Southwark Playhouse) and *Splinters* (Talawa TC).

Dawn was awarded the Jerwood Young Directors award at the Young Vic and was formerly Resident Assistant Director at the Royal Court. Dawn is the Artistic Director of Mamamissi Productions.

SOUTRA GILMOUR DESIGNER

Soutra's theatre credits include:
When The World Was Green (Young Vic Theatre); *Animal* (Soho Theatre and tour); *Through the Leaves* (Southwark Playhouse and West End); *The Flu Season*, *Les Justes* and *Witness* (The Gate); *The Shadow of a Boy* (RNT); *Sun is Shining* (59e59, New York); *Hand in Hand* (Hampstead Theatre); *The Birthday Party* (The Crucible); *Fool For Love* (English Touring Theatre); *The Woman Who Swallowed a Pin* and *The Winter's Tale* (Southwark Playhouse); *Antigone and Therese Raquin* (Citizens Theatre); *Tear From a Glass Eye* (Gate and National Studio); *Peter Pan* (Tramway, Glasgow); *The Mayor of Zalamea* and *The Kindness of Strangers* (Liverpool Everyman); *Ghost City* (59e59, New York) and *Country Music* (Royal Court).

Opera includes: *The Girl of Sand* (Almeida Theatre); *Corridors* (ENO Bayliss Project); *A Better Place* (ENO Coliseum); *La Bohème* (Opera Ireland); *El Cimmarrón* (Queen Elizabeth Hall); *Bathtime* (ENO Studio) and *Eight Songs For A Mad King* (National and world tour).

Film includes: *The Follower* and *Amazing Grace*.

NATASHA CHIVERS
LIGHTING DESIGNER

Natasha's recent theatre work includes: *The Kindness of Strangers* (Liverpool Everyman); *Ma Rainey's Black Bottom* and *The Entertainer* (Liverpool Playhouse); *Compact Failure* (Clean Break Tour); *The Straits* (59 East 59, New York Paines Plough, Hampstead Theatre); *Very Little Women* (Lip Service tour); *On Blindness* (Paines Plough, Frantic Assembly, Graeae); *The Birthday Party* (Tag Theatre Company); *The Cherry Orchard* and *After The Dance* (Oxford Stage Company national tour); *The Bomb-itty of Errors* (The New Ambassadors), *Playhouse Creatures* (West Yorkshire Playhouse); *Peepshow* (Frantic Assembly, Plymouth Theatre Royal, Lyric Hammersmith and tour); *Wit* and *The Memory Of Water* (Stellar Quines, Tron, Traverse and tour); (Present Laughter (Bath Theatre Royal Productions); *The Drowned World* (Paines Plough, Traverse Theatre and Bush Theatre); *Tiny Dynamite* (Frantic Assembly, Paines Plough, Lyric Hammersmith and tour); and *A Chaste Maid In Cheapside* (Almeida Theatre and tour).

COMPANY

SEAN PRITCHARD
SOUND DESIGNER

Sean is from Liverpool and studied Production and Performance Technology at The Liverpool Institute for Performing Arts before taking a job with the Everyman Theatre in 1999. He is currently Chief Technician at the Everyman.

Sound designs for the company include: *The Kindness of Strangers*; *Fly*; *The Mayor of Zalamea*; *A Little Pinch of Chilli* and *'Master Harold'... and the Boys.*

MARIE JONES
COSTUME SUPERVISOR

Marie studied fashion and then moved on to Theatre Costume Interpretation at Mable Fletcher College. Marie's work as a freelance costumier has included costumes for Oldham Coliseum, the Royal Exchange, West Yorkshire Playhouse, Jimmy McGovern's film *Liam* and the creation of many panto dames to have appeared on the Everyman stage over the last few years. She has worked extensively at the Liverpool Everyman and Playhouse, most recently: *Breezeblock Park*, *The Entertainer*, The Noël Coward Double Bill, *Ma Rainey's Black Bottom*, *Fly* and *The Anniversary*.

Marie other projects include: Brouhaha International Street Festival, Working Class Hero on the recent Imagine DVD, costume supervisor for many shows at LIPA, the Splash project for MYPT and *Twopence To Cross the Mersey* at the Liverpool Empire.

SUPPORT US

The Liverpool Everyman and Playhouse are in the midst of a creative revolution: more new productions are now created here in Liverpool and there are more opportunities for talented writers and actors to be nurtured through our new writing and community initiatives. There is also a stronger presence of quality theatre on the city's cultural map and a higher profile on the national and international stage.

Our funding bodies and our audiences provide the grassroots support which ensures our survival, and we are sincerely grateful for it. But if we are to fulfil our ambitions for these theatres to flourish and blossom for future generations, we must be imaginative in raising support.

With your help, we can go further than these theatres have ever gone before.

By supporting the Everyman and Playhouse you will make it possible for us to create more spectacular work on both our stages; to nurture a new generation of actors and writers' to bring the best theatre makers to our city; to take Liverpool theatre far beyond home turf; and to reach out to our communities so that theatre can touch the lives of everyone on Merseyside.

For more details of how you as an individual, or your company, can be part of the growth and success of theatre in Liverpool, please see our website at www.everymanplayhouse.com, or contact our Development Department on 0151 706 9115 or at development@everymanplayhouse.com

Liverpool Everyman and Playhouse would like to thank all our current supporters:

FUNDERS

  The City of Liverpool KNOWSLEY METROPOLITAN BOROUGH Sefton Council Metropolitan Borough of Wirral

CORPORATE SPONSORS
Benson Signs; Bibby Factors Northwest Ltd; Brabners Chaffe Street; C3 Imaging; Chadwick Chartered Accountants; Dawsons Music Ltd; Duncan Sheard Glass; DWF Solicitors; Grant Thornton; Hope Street Hotel; HSBC Bank Plc; John Lewis; Mando Group; Nonconform Design; Nviron Ltd; Oddbins; Synergy Colour Printing; The Famous Bankrupt Shop; The Workbank.

TRUSTS & GRANT-MAKING BODIES
BBC Northern Exposure; BBC Radio Merseyside; The Eleanor Rathbone Charitable Trust; Five; The Granada Foundation; Liverpool Culture Company; P H Holt Charitable Trust.

INDIVIDUAL SUPPORTERS
Peter and Geraldine Bounds, George C Carver, Councillor Eddie Clein, Mr & Mrs Dan Hugo, A. Thomas Jackson, Ms D. Leach, Frank D Paterson, Les Read, Sheena Streather, DB Williams and all those who prefer to remain anonymous.

 Liverpool Everyman and Playhouse is a registered charity no: 1081229
www.everymanplayhouse.com

STAFF

URBAN LEGEND

First published in 2004 by Oberon Books Ltd
521 Caledonian Road, London N7 9RH
Tel: 020 7607 3637 / Fax: 020 7607 3629
e-mail: oberon.books@btinternet.com
www.oberonbooks.com

A catalogue record for this book is available from the British
Library.

ISBN: 1 84002 490 9

Printed in Great Britain by Antony Rowe Ltd, Chippenham.

Characters

HORSE
Late sixties/early seventies. Tall, broad shouldered, potbelly, long white curly hair. His body has the slack look of wasted muscle. Born and bread in Bootle. Hasn't worked since he was forty, when he had an undiagnosed breakdown. Was a boxer, as well as a labourer. Has a taste for cheap cider.

ROBBIE
Thirty-nine. Horse's eldest son. Used to be a small time crook. Considers himself retired at forty. Been on Job Seekers Allowance for years. He is smaller than his father but strong. Drinks too much but not yet an alcoholic.

WAYNE
Seventeen. The loss of his mother has been very hard on him. He is a self-taught musician, playing guitar and able to compose his own songs of which he has many. Wants to be a successful singer/song writer. Has a problem with pot addiction, and uses a bucket to smoke it, which makes his addiction ten times worse than a joint smoker. He is small for his age, but very handsome. His hair is longish and dark brown.

BOBBO
Thirty-nine. Small and skinny, with a shaved head and missing teeth. He is a professional parasite. Was a heroin addict as a younger man but got himself off it. Cocaine and beer is his poison now. He has a way about him that is instantly likeable.

Dedication

This work is dedicated to Amelia Stephens, Suzanne Bell, Deborah Aydon, Gemma Bodinetz and Dawn Walton, who have all been instrumental in the forming of the play.

Special Thanks

A special thank you goes to the Liverpool Everyman and Playhouse Theatres, and everyone who works for them.

ACT ONE

Scene 1: Egg Men

Music – 'Every Night' by Paul McCartney.

It is in the middle of a very hot summer. Cross-section of a flat in a high-rise at Bootle in North Liverpool. Centre stage is a living room, the wall paper was once of a purple and green floral design, which has so much nicotine staining on it that it has become a sort of gangrenous colour. There are two couches over on stage right: one follows the back wall line, the other the side wall. They are rotten and looked to have been rescued from skips only to be reduced to an even more decrepit and battered state by their new owners. There is a coverless duvet on the one against the back wall: it too is filthy, covered in old tea stains and dirt; someone is under it. In front of the two couches is a low coffee table, covered in ash, joint stumps, cigarette buts, empty skin packets, dead and alive matches, lighters, burnt-down candles whose melted wax has joined with some of this clutter, and a bucket of water with a bottle standing in it. The floor is carpeted, a pale green, but spilt drinks and the like have made it mostly brown and is littered with, silver foil pie dishes, newspapers, empty cans of special brew and other rubbish. Over stage left there is an old TV set with three older looking videos and a game console surrounding it. Behind the TV set is a large window. On the back wall behind the couch is a serving hatch and further over still a door, which leads to the hall. Further stage right is a small bedroom, which is in darkness. It has a window on the right hand wall and a door in the back wall over on the left hand wall. There is a noise off stage left, the sound of a toilet being flushed and then a moment or so later the door to the living room opens and man walks in. He is in his late sixties, he is fairly tall, with a big potbelly, His hair is white and quite long and curly; he has a vest and boxer shorts on. He has an unopened can of cider in one hand. He seems to be searching for something in the room; he picks odd things up, such as spoons from discarded soup bowls and puts them in his underwear pockets. After a few moments he walks over to the vacant couch and plonks himself on it; he looks at the coffee table, and then rummages around on it before plucking up a remote control from the mess. He aims it at the telly but nothing happens. He opens a can of cider, takes a sip and then gets up, leans over toward the telly, reaches the remote out to toward it and tries again. Nothing. He then throws the remote at the sleeping figure under the duvet, it bounces off his head with a dull thud. Music fades.

WAYNE: Eh! What are yer doin?

HORSE: Remote's not workin.

WAYNE: What?

HORSE: The remote.

WAYNE: Yer what?

HORSE: It won't work.

WAYNE: 'Ave yer just got up?

HORSE: Switch it on fer on us will yer kid?

WAYNE: What did yer last slave die of?

HORSE: (*Beat.*) I'm 'ungry.

WAYNE: Can't yer make yerself some toast?

HORSE: Woman's job.

WAYNE: I'm not a fuckin woman.

HORSE: Yer cook don't yer?

WAYNE: No.

HORSE: I've seen yer.

WAYNE: Only cos I 'ad to.

HORSE: Do us an egg, go on.

WAYNE: I can't do eggs.

HORSE: It's easy kid.

WAYNE: You do one then.

HORSE: Do I look like a woman?

WAYNE: Do I?

HORSE: I'll pay yer?

WAYNE: 'Ow much?

HORSE: A quid.

WAYNE: Yer 'aven't got any money.

HORSE: I 'ave.

WAYNE: I'll do it fer a fiver.

HORSE: A fiver fer an egg, what did it come out of a Bronchitis?

WAYNE: A what?

HORSE: Dinosaur.

WAYNE: What are yer on about Grandad?

HORSE: I'm starvin 'ere me.

WAYNE: Go 'ed, a quid then.

HORSE: A nice boiled egg kid, on a bit of toast.

WAYNE: Right, I'll just do a bucket first.

HORSE: And can yer cut it into soldiers.

WAYNE: Do what?

HORSE: Me toast, cut it into little soldiers.

WAYNE: I'll just sort me 'ead out first Grandad. (*Pause.*) I 'ope it's not gonna stay this 'ot all day.

> *WAYNE gets a lump of resin from in his left sock. He takes the chalice from on top of the bottle and puts it on the coffee table in front of him, he then takes a lighter and starts to burn the resin; he then crumbles some into the chalice. Once he has put a fair bit in, he screws the chalice back onto the bottle and lights the lighter once more, hovers the naked flame*

over it and slowly at first, pulls the bottle up out of the water, which causes a vacuum inside it, which sucks the flame through the chalice, lighting the cannabis resin, and filling the bottle with a fair volume of smoke. WAYNE then unscrews the chalice and inhales all of the smoke from out of the bottle. He holds it in for a second, and then exhales it all in a long stream, which blasts across the room.

HORSE: Takin yer life away that bucket kid.

WAYNE: It's only weed.

HORSE: Not the way you do it, I've seen yer droolin after three of dem.

WAYNE: What else am I supposed to do?

HORSE: There's a big wide world out there fer yer to explore, jobs to be 'ad.

WAYNE: There's an even bigger world inside 'ere.

WAYNE taps his skull.

HORSE: Where's me egg?

WAYNE: I'll sort yer now.

WAYNE gets up and stumbles toward the kitchen. We see him through the hatch.

What do yer do?

HORSE: Boil it.

WAYNE: 'Ow?

HORSE: In a pan.

WAYNE: Right.

WAYNE takes a pan from the sink shelf and puts it on one of the rings and then turns the ring on, he then takes an egg from the fridge and puts it in the empty pan.

'Ow long for?

HORSE: Long enough to cook it.

WAYNE: Sorted.

HORSE: What are yer doin with yerself today then?

WAYNE: Nothin.

HORSE: It's goin to be a scorcher again.

WAYNE: I don't like the sun.

HORSE: Yer Mum did. She used to love sitting in the sun getting a tan.

WAYNE: Are yer goin to see Nan today Grandad?

HORSE: Me legs are bad kid.

HORSE picks up the remote and tries again.

WAYNE: You haven't been…

HORSE: (*Cutting in.*) What's the knack with this again?

WAYNE: (*Beat.*) You've got to squeeze the batteries at the same time as yer press a button.

HORSE: Do what?

WAYNE: Squeeze them in at the back.

HORSE tries and nothing happens.

HORSE: Japanese crap.

WAYNE: Won't it work?

HORSE: They make everythin so that it dies on yer. They could make things last fer almost ever, if they wanted to.

WAYNE: Who?

HORSE: The Japs.

WAYNE: Yeah?

HORSE: But they don't, they give everything a heart life, so many beats and then the lights go out. (*Muttered.*) Fuckin Lizards…

WAYNE: Is it switched on at the wall?

HORSE: I can't see from 'ere.

WAYNE: That might be it.

HORSE: What's the point in turnin it off at the wall?

WAYNE: I don't know; Me Da does it sometimes.

HORSE: Why can't 'e just leave it on standby, that's what it's for?

WAYNE: Save money.

HORSE: We're on the bloody fiddle aren't we? No, 'e does it to wind me up.

WAYNE: 'E doesn't.

HORSE: I'm tellin yer Wayne; 'e's tryin to wind me up so I'll move out.

WAYNE: Nah.

HORSE: 'E is.

WAYNE: (*Joke.*) Stop smokin crack Grandad.

HORSE: Tellin yer.

WAYNE: 'E just wants yer to see more of Nan. (*Pause.*) When are yer gonna see 'er?

HORSE: I want all me soldiers to 'ave little red 'ats.

WAYNE: (*Puzzled.*) Yer what?

HORSE: When yer do me toasted soldiers make sure they all 'ave little red 'ats.

WAYNE: Little red 'ats, 'ow?

HORSE: Blob of tomato sauce on one end of each of 'em.

WAYNE: Yer kiddin?

HORSE: Don't over do it, I want little caps, not busbies.

WAYNE: Is that all yer want?

HORSE: Yer can rub some of that gunk I got off the doctor into me legs while that's cookin.

WAYNE: I've only just got up.

HORSE: Come on kid, I can't do it with me arthritis or I wouldn't ask.

WAYNE: It stinks.

HORSE: I wouldn't ask yer if I could do it meself.

WAYNE: It's too 'ot fer all that.

HORSE: What about all the things I do fer yer.

WAYNE: What things?

HORSE: I got yer that vid didn't I?

WAYNE: What vid?

HORSE: The dirty one.

WAYNE: *Emmanuelle Three?*

HORSE: That's the one.

WAYNE: It wasn't exactly hard-core Grandad, I've seen more goin on in an episode of *Buffy the Vampire Slayer.*

HORSE: If I'd 'ave seen that at your age I'd 'ave never bin off the Vaseline.

WAYNE: Shut up.

HORSE: What more d'yer want?

WAYNE: A lot.

HORSE: The tins on the telly.

WAYNE comes back into the living room and picks up the tin and opens it. He wrinkles his nose at the smell. He looks at the unappetizing sight of HORSE.

WAYNE: 'Ave yer 'ad a wash?

HORSE: Course I 'ave.

WAYNE goes and kneels at his Grandad's feet and he starts to rub the oil into his legs.

Not so rough.

WAYNE: I'm not a fuckin *mass-sewer* yer know!

HORSE: No wonder yer can't keep a bird.

WAYNE: I didn't think I was koppin off.

HORSE: Well yer'd 'ave no chance with me with them clumsy mitts.

WAYNE: If yer was a chick I'd slow down but yer not so I won't cos I wanna get it over with as soon as possible; alright?

HORSE: Well make sure yer don't miss any.

WAYNE: I'm tryin Grandad but when you've got as many lumps as you 'ave it's 'ard to get into all the corners like yer know what I mean?

HORSE: Ow! Watch it, you'll 'ave me varicose veins jettin off.

WAYNE: Arh 'ere are, that'll 'ave to do yer!

WAYNE jumps up.

HORSE: That's better.

WAYNE: Good.

HORSE: Smells like a beggar's bell end like.

WAYNE: Tell me about it.

HORSE: But it'll do the job.

There is the sound of a lift rattling in its travels, from outside the flat.

WAYNE: That'll be Dad.

HORSE: As long as e's got me cans.

There is the noise of somebody opening the front door from off stage.

ROBBIE comes into the living room carting a plastic bag; he is livid.

ROBBIE: Cheeky fuckin bastards.

HORSE: What's up?

ROBBIE: (*Pacing.*) That's it now, that's fuckin it now.

WAYNE: (*Through hatch.*) What is?

ROBBIE: They're stoppin me dole.

HORSE: What for?

ROBBIE: Tryin to put me on that New Deal thing.

HORSE: A what?

ROBBIE: Fuckin New Deal! What does he think 'e is, a fuckin dealer? Thinks e's gonna do a deal with me? 'E's just some little kid.

HORSE: Who?

ROBBIE: The lad who signs me on.

HORSE: What's the New Deal?

ROBBIE: What was wrong with the fuckin auld one? That's what I wanna fuckin know. Come in, sign on, fuck off; mind yer own business.

HORSE: What do they want from yer now?

ROBBIE: You've gotta go in once a week instead of every two and then this little tit just out of school does a thing on his computer and the next Salute, 'e's got a job that you've gotta go for.

WAYNE: Don't yer wanna job Dad?

ROBBIE: Don't you fuckin start an all, I've done my hard

graft, I've fuckin done my bit, I'm retired me, I'm not a well man. You should be supporting us. What's up with yer? (*Beat.*) I've told yer I know lads who can get yer work. Good money, cash in 'and, no questions asked. Zip, bang, bling bling, all that one.

HORSE: On the frag?

ROBBIE: On the frag.

WAYNE: I don't wanna work on no scrap metal shredder.

ROBBIE: Beneath yer is it?

HORSE: Bad fer yer lungs that game, Robbie.

ROBBIE: 'E could just do it fer a couple of months.

WAYNE: Why don't you?

ROBBIE: I've just told yer.

WAYNE: Why have they stopped yer money?

ROBBIE: Only goes and gets me a job up on the screen today, doesn't 'e eh?

WAYNE: What was it?

ROBBIE: Shit house attendant.

HORSE: Yer jokin?

ROBBIE: I'm not jokin, and 'e knew I wasn't fuckin jokin when I lifted the prick over the counter.

WAYNE: No way.

ROBBIE: 'E's lucky, I was gonna bite 'is nose off.

WAYNE: Why didn't yer?

ROBBIE: Blackheads.

WAYNE: What did yer do?

ROBBIE: Threw 'im back.

HORSE: What 'appened then?

ROBBIE: Security got on me case and they kicked me out.

HORSE: Can't yer go back and…

ROBBIE: And what? Apologise and say, 'Course I'll sit in a little room in a shit house, like some fuckin Menk, mate.' Get a grip, I'm not doin that, I don't even wanna fuckin job, I'm retired me, but if I did, I'd be choosin me own, not havin some wanker with tissue at the side of his bed, plottin me life out fer me.

HORSE: I warned yer about all this.

ROBBIE: Who did?

HORSE: I said it right from the beginning.

ROBBIE: What?

HORSE: It's all your fuckin man's work, this yer know?

ROBBIE: What are yer on about?

HORSE: Tony Blair.

ROBBIE: 'E's not me fuckin man.

HORSE: You've changed yer tune.

ROBBIE: Well if I've changed me tune, 'e's playin in a different fuckin band.

HORSE: I can't believe yer voted fer him.

ROBBIE: I only voted fer him in me 'ead, I didn't actually go down and put me thing in the box.

HORSE: Same thing.

ROBBIE: Is it fuck!

HORSE: I'm tellin yer he's the Anti-Christ that one.

ROBBIE: 'E's off.

HORSE: 'Im and his cowboy partner.

ROBBIE: Get a grip Dad.

HORSE: Couple of God 'eads.

ROBBIE: This is all I need.

HORSE: 'E's losin it now though in he?

ROBBIE: Who?

HORSE: (*Spits it out.*) The Family Man.

WAYNE: What are yer gonna do Dad?

HORSE: Seen 'ow much 'e's aged in only a few years...

WAYNE: Eh Dad?

HORSE: Same thing 'appened to Hitler, aged ten years in only a few months.

WAYNE: Dad?

HORSE: They say it's the burden of great pressure.

WAYNE: Dad?

HORSE: But it's not; it's the fuckin price they pay fer sleepin with the Devil. Either that or their masks are shit.

ROBBIE: (*Shouts.*) Dad, just shut the fuck up fer a minute about all yer David Icke crap. I just need to think this through. (*Pause.*) What's that smell?

WAYNE: What smell?

ROBBIE: Are you cookin somethin?

WAYNE: Yeah.

HORSE: 'E's doin me an egg.

WAYNE: Boiled.

ROBBIE: Show us the pan.

WAYNE comes into the living room with the pan.

ROBBIE: What the fuck's that?

WAYNE: What does it look like?

ROBBIE: It looks suspiciously like a very 'ot egg in an even 'otter empty pan.

WAYNE: I'm doin 'im a boiled egg.

ROBBIE: With no water?

WAYNE: Does it need water?

HORSE: 'Aven't yer put water in?

WAYNE: Yer never said.

ROBBIE: I can't believe you came from my fuckin loins sometimes Wayne.

WAYNE: Whatever.

ROBBIE: Throw it out the window it fuckin stinks.

WAYNE: Don't yer want it Grandad?

HORSE: I'm not 'ungry now kid.

WAYNE: Can I still 'ave me quid.

ROBBIE: What quid?

WAYNE: 'E's said 'e'd give me a quid if I done 'im an egg.

ROBBIE: Wayne, I'm gonna fuckin lose it in a minute.

WAYNE: I'm only tryin to help.

ROBBIE: Do us a bucket.

WAYNE: A bucket?

ROBBIE: That's what I said.

WAYNE: Nah.

ROBBIE: You what?

WAYNE: Yer can't 'andle them.

ROBBIE: Who can't?

WAYNE: You can't.

ROBBIE: Says who?

WAYNE: 'Ave one of yer cans.

ROBBIE: Me 'ead's kettled 'ere Wayne, now sort us a bucket.

WAYNE moves over to the bucket and rapidly starts to make it up.

ROBBIE: Do yer know what, I could kick that prick's 'ead off the little nerd. Looked like 'is ma 'ad dressed 'im. I should wait fer 'im to clock off.

HORSE: Yeah well, that's not goin to do yer any good is it?

ROBBIE: What is, eh Dad? What's gonna do me some good, crawlin back down there on me 'ands and knees and offer 'im a wank?

HORSE: You've got to play the game Robbie, yer know that.

ROBBIE: I don't play games. You know that.

HORSE: You've got to make money Robbie.

ROBBIE: What like you did?

HORSE: You know what…

ROBBIE: Provide a palace fer yer kids did yer eh Dad? Set us up fer life?

HORSE: I got ripped off, I…

ROBBIE: You gave up, gave up good and early.

HORSE: I lost everythin; I couldn't start again.

ROBBIE: Couldn't or wouldn't.

HORSE: I couldn't go back in the ring; I was too old.

ROBBIE: Yer could've worked a door or somethin.

HORSE: I'd 'ad enough of usin these.

HORSE shows ROBBIE his large fists. They are shaking.

ROBBIE: Lost yer bottle yer mean.

HORSE lowers his fists. His son has hit a nerve. They stare at each other for a moment.

We 'ad nothin thanks to you.

HORSE looks away.

WAYNE has finished building up the bucket.

WAYNE: Dad?

ROBBIE: What?

WAYNE: 'Ere.

ROBBIE: Put more in.

WAYNE: More?

ROBBIE: Do it.

WAYNE starts to add some more resin to the chalice.

WAYNE: You'll cough.

ROBBIE: I won't.

WAYNE: Yer will.

ROBBIE: So what's it to you?

WAYNE: Well don't start on me when yer can't stop coughin.

ROBBIE: 'Aven't yer done it yet.

WAYNE: Go 'ed.

ROBBIE: Light it.

WAYNE lights the blow and pulls the bottle up.

WAYNE: 'Ere.

ROBBIE ignores his father and instead heads for the bottle; he removes the chalice and quickly inhales all the smoke.

There is a beat and ROBBIE exhales, and then he starts to cough. It is a painful, shrill, hacking cough.

ROBBIE: Jesus! (*Continues to cough.*)

HORSE: Is 'e gonna be alright?

WAYNE: I told him.

HORSE: Get 'im some water.

WAYNE: Do yer want some water Dad?

ROBBIE: Urgh God. (*Still coughing.*)

HORSE: I can't see the point in that.

WAYNE: Yer get used to 'em.

ROBBIE can't stop coughing and leaves the room for the toilet.

HORSE: Like a gas attack that.

WAYNE: What?

HORSE: Weapon of mass destruction one of those. You'll 'ave the fuckin inspectors around. Last thing 'e needs that on top of what's just 'appened Wayne.

WAYNE: 'E asked fer it.

HORSE: 'E wants to grow up and smell the tea. You'll never blag me into 'avin another one of dem, I thought me 'ead was rollin around on the ceilin.

WAYNE: Yer just not hard-core enough.

HORSE: I'm not stupid enough more like. It doesn't even smell like it did in my day lad.

WAYNE: What, weed?

HORSE: (*Ominous.*) The Lizards 'ave got at it.

WAYNE: Your off yer 'ead.

HORSE: They know the artists smoke pot, so they've

tampered with it, put somethin in it that makes sure yer art stays on yer bedroom wall or inside yer skull or whatevever.

WAYNE: Stop smoking crack.

HORSE: I'm telling yer. They're probably making it all up in big vats on Jacko's ranch, that Neverland place.

WAYNE: There is no Lizards Granddad.

HORSE: Yes there is.

WAYNE: Seen one first 'and 'ave yer?

HORSE looks troubled and tries the remote again, before slamming it down.

HORSE: Pass us a can will yer?

WAYNE takes a can from the plastic bag that ROBBIE brought in and he passes it to his Grandad. They are quiet for a moment, as WAYNE builds himself another bucket.

ROBBIE can still be heard coughing in the bathroom.

WAYNE: What's gonna 'appen now.

HORSE: 'Ow do yer mean?

WAYNE: We'll lose the flat fer a start.

HORSE: It's just a flat.

WAYNE: Maybe to you it is.

HORSE: We won't lose it, 'e's not gonna let that 'appen is 'e?

WAYNE: What's 'e gonna do then?

HORSE: 'E'll do somethin, we've gotta eat.

WAYNE: I dunno yer know.

HORSE: 'E'll have to pull himself together and get a job; 'e's got mates, who can sort 'im out.

WAYNE: 'E won't work.

HORSE: What about you?

WAYNE: What about me?

HORSE: Maybe this is the kick up the arse yer need kid. You could be the breadwinner, show 'im up.

WAYNE: Nah.

HORSE: What do yer mean, nah?

WAYNE: I can't.

HORSE: Can't?

WAYNE: You 'eard.

HORSE: Can't what Wayne?

WAYNE: Get a job.

HORSE: Why?

WAYNE: Because.

HORSE: That's not good enough.

WAYNE: Don't start on me Grandad.

HORSE: Don't yer want money, a career.

WAYNE ignores him and ignites his lighter and hovers it over the chalice.

What's 'appened to the youths of today eh?

WAYNE pulls up his bucket.

WAYNE: I've got me songs.

HORSE: Taste nice do they?

WAYNE: I'm just not ready.

WAYNE inhales the smoke.

HORSE: Yer can't sing more like.

WAYNE exhales.

WAYNE: I can.

HORSE: Yer can't lad, yer watch these fuckin programmes, where they turn ordinary kids into stars and you think it's goin to 'appen to you.

WAYNE: I don't. I've got talent, I can write songs.

HORSE: Yer can't write music.

WAYNE: Make it up then and remember it.

HORSE: Well that's all well and good as an 'obby kid. But you can't be somethin yer not. And yer know what I'm sayin don't yer?

WAYNE: No.

HORSE: Yer not 'er Wayne.

WAYNE: What?

HORSE: Yer not yer Mother. (*Pause.*) She 'ad the voice of an angel, she had that…thing…and even then… Your talents lie elsewhere.

WAYNE: What do you know?

HORSE: Chase a dream like that kid and you'll never be 'appy.

ROBBIE re-enters. He looks like shit.

ROBBIE: Jesus, that caught in me throat that one.

WAYNE: I told yer.

ROBBIE: 'Ave I got snot in me 'air.

WAYNE: Snot?

ROBBIE: 'Ave I or 'aven't I?

WAYNE: I can't see none.

ROBBIE: It's got a bad taste that blow.

WAYNE: Yer reckon.

ROBBIE: Like petrol or somethin.

HORSE: It's the Lizards.

ROBBIE: (*To WAYNE.*) As 'e 'ad one.

HORSE: Do I look like an idiot?

WAYNE: Passive smokin.

HORSE: There's nothing passive about me lad.

ROBBIE: Are you goin to see Nan today?

HORSE: Me legs Son.

ROBBIE: 'Ave yer been takin yer cod livers.

HORSE: No.

ROBBIE: Why not?

HORSE: 'Aven't 'ad time.

ROBBIE: 'Aven't 'ad time?

HORSE: That's what I said.

ROBBIE: When are yer gonna go and see 'er.

HORSE: When are you?

ROBBIE: She's your wife.

HORSE: She's your mother.

ROBBIE: I'll get up there.

Pause.

WAYNE: Dad?

ROBBIE: What?

WAYNE: One of me strings 'as broke on me guitar.

ROBBIE: Yer what?

WAYNE: One of me strings 'as snapped.

ROBBIE: Well it'll be easier to play then won't it?

WAYNE: 'Ow d'yer work that one out like?

ROBBIE: Less strings, less things fer yer fingers to do.

WAYNE: Can yer get us some new ones?

ROBBIE: Are you for fuckin real or what?

WAYNE: What?

ROBBIE: I've just 'ad me money stopped Wayne; I don't know where yer fuckin next meal's comin from and yer askin me to buy yer guitar strings!

WAYNE: Sorry.

ROBBIE: I mean Christ Wayne.

WAYNE: I'm sorry, I just…

ROBBIE: I don't know what the fuck I'm gonna do 'ere.

WAYNE: Are we gonna lose the flat Dad?

ROBBIE: No.

WAYNE: What are yer gonna do?

ROBBIE: I'm gonna go out, and I'm gonna 'it every boozer I come across from 'ere to town, and I'm gonna wet me whistle until I fuckin gargle when I talk, and then when I come back, I'll know what I'm gonna do.

ROBBIE storms out.

WAYNE gets up and goes over to the television, he switches on the game console that is over there and then the television. Then he sits back down to wait for the game to load.

HORSE: I don't like the mood 'e's in.

WAYNE: I 'ate the way you've got to wait fer these things to get goin.

HORSE: Don't 'ave it on loud.

WAYNE picks up the remote and turns the sound down.

WAYNE: It's not as good with the sound down yer can't 'ear no one creepin up on yer.

HORSE: The news is on in a minute.

WAYNE: (*To machine.*) Come on I wanna kick ass.

HORSE: Yer could do with a kick up yer *ass* yer mean.

HORSE smells himself. He gets up and looks around the room.

HORSE: 'Ave yer seen any clean washin around?

WAYNE: 'Ang on. I'm on. (*The game has started.*)

HORSE: Didn't ' yer Dad bring a bag 'ome the other day.

WAYNE: (*At game.*) Fuck.

HORSE: What?

WAYNE: That was lucky?

HORSE: What was?

WAYNE: Car nearly flipped.

HORSE looks at the screen.

HORSE: Are you in that car?

WAYNE: Yeah, but I can get out though if I want.

HORSE: I'm sure 'e went the launderette, 'e was askin me fer fifty pees.

WAYNE: 'Ere are look, see me get out the car.

HORSE: Need something fresh on.

WAYNE: See that old woman there Grandad.

WAYNE points to the screen.

HORSE: Where?

WAYNE: She's only tiny cos she's way in the distance, but get on this.

HORSE: What?

WAYNE: Get me sniper rifle out, point it at 'er; zoom right in. See 'er now? See 'er 'ead dead big in the lens?

HORSE: That's good in'it.

WAYNE: Get on this.

WAYNE blows the old woman's head off with one shot.

HORSE: What the fuck?

WAYNE: Blew 'er 'ead right off.

HORSE: What for?

WAYNE: Mad in'it?

HORSE: What did she do to you?

WAYNE: Nothin.

HORSE: So that's a game where you blow old women's 'eads off.

WAYNE: No, you've got do all kinds of other things, that's just something yer can do, if yer want, yer don't get no points fer it or nothing, and if yer do it to much yer get coppers on yer case.

HORSE: What kind of a game is that?

WAYNE: Top game this Grandad.

HORSE: It's fuckin sick.

WAYNE: Stop smokin crack.

HORSE: Can yer do that in the game as well?

WAYNE: What?

HORSE: Smoke crack?

WAYNE: Nah, yer can fuck prostitutes though.

HORSE: You what?

WAYNE: Yeah, just drive up to them and they get in the car after a bit and yer drive of to a quiet spot and she gives it to yer. Yer get 'ealth fer it.

HORSE: 'Ealth? Fuckin bad fer the 'ealth more like it.

WAYNE: Everyone plays this.

HORSE: Turn it off.

WAYNE: What?

HORSE: You 'eard.

WAYNE: It's not real.

HORSE: Off!!!

WAYNE: Alright.

WAYNE goes over to the console and turns it off.

HORSE: Fuckin Lizard's game that.

WAYNE: Whatever.

HORSE: You wanna 'ave some fuckin respect fer yer elders.

WAYNE: She wasn't real.

HORSE: Get out of me sight.

WAYNE: What?

HORSE: Go to yer room.

WAYNE: Get a grip.

HORSE stands, he is shaking.

HORSE: GET OUT!

WAYNE leaves the room.

HORSE walks over to the console and fiddles with it, he manages to get the eject system to work by chance, and takes out the game disk. He glares at it.

HORSE: Fuckin Lizards!

HORSE throws the game out of the window. He flops down onto a couch and looks at his shaking hands.

Music – 'Helter Skelter' by The Beatles.

Fade to blackout.

Scene 2: The barnacle

The Living Room. Just gone mid-night, the same day. The door opens and in falls ROBBIE and another man. They are extremely drunk and in high spirits. The man is BOBBO; he is wearing a T-shirt, tracksuit bottoms and trainers. He has a bottle of suspect looking vodka in his right hand. ROBBIE has two plastic bags seemingly full of cans.

Music fades.

BOBBO: Yer haven't decorated since I was last 'ere then?

ROBBIE: What are yer on about yer cheeky bastard; only did it the other week.

BOBBO: What did it say on the paint can? Grunge?

ROBBIE: Yer know where the door is.

BOBBO: Yeah, behind the bin bags.

ROBBIE: We 'ad some fuckin laughs in 'ere though, didn't we?

BOBBO: Best days of me life Robbie, best days of me life.

ROBBIE: Yeah?

BOBBO: Tellin yer.

ROBBIE: You don't have to tell me, I know.

BOBBO: Are yer on it?

ROBBIE: I'm on it Bobbo.

BOBBO: Been a few years 'asn't it?

ROBBIE: Four or five mate.

BOBBO: Long time.

ROBBIE: I can't believe I bumped into yer, I never go out.

BOBBO: I know yeah.

ROBBIE: What 'appened to yer mate in the suit?

BOBBO: Got rid of 'im when yer said come back.

ROBBIE: 'Ow come?

BOBBO: 'E's just some prick whose 'ead I'm blaggin.

ROBBIE: Oh aye?

BOBBO: Been on 'is plastic all night.

ROBBIE: 'Ow'd yer manage that?

BOBBO: That'd be tellin.

ROBBIE: Come on.

BOBBO: Get on this.

ROBBIE: Go 'ed.

BOBBO: Bumped into 'im a few months ago right.

ROBBIE: Yeah.

BOBBO: 'E was in the Jaw Bone, really pissed.

ROBBIE: Really?

BOBBO: Really.

ROBBIE: Disgustin.

BOBBO: I'll second that.

BOBBO takes a large swig from the dodgy vodka bottle.

ROBBIE: I'll third it.

ROBBIE holds his hand out for the drink to be thrown and BOBBO throws it and ROBBIE catches it clumsily. He takes a swig.

BOBBO: I mean 'e's proper pissed and the managers gettin close to throwin 'im out.

ROBBIE: Sure this is proper vodka?

BOBBO: Yeah. So I goes the bar meself like and we gets talkin and that and I makes 'im laugh a couple of times; few jokes, witty comments, whatever, and 'e starts buyin me drinks.

ROBBIE: 'E's not queer is 'e?

BOBBO: No, alls 'e can go on about is 'ow 'is wife's left 'im; just took off out the blue.

ROBBIE: Lovely.

BOBBO: Oh beautiful mate, beautiful. So 'e's buyin the drinks and I'm listen to 'im and 'e likes that. But while I'm listen me eyes are all over 'is wallet every time it comes out the fuckin pocket.

ROBBIE: Chunky?

BOBBO: It wasn't full of cash, I mean 'e 'ad some, but it was full of plastic, some of it gold.

ROBBIE: Nice.

BOBBO: Very nice Robbie, very nice indeed. Anyway I've 'ad a good free load off 'im like and I'm well tanked up, but me 'ead's workin over time like but 'e 'ands it to me on a plate anyway.

ROBBIE: What, 'is wallet?

BOBBO: As good as.

ROBBIE: I don't get yer.

BOBBO: No one ever does Robbie. No, 'e threw up, right on the bar, bit splashed on me, bit splashed on the manager and we're out on our arses right.

ROBBIE: Yeah.

BOBBO: So, I mean 'e can 'ardly talk 'e's that bevied, but 'e's dead apologetic, pukin on me and gettin me thrown out me local and ruinin me night, all that caper.

ROBBIE: Did it stink?

BOBBO: What the sick?

ROBBIE: Yeah.

BOBBO: Reeked, so 'e was proper and appropriately sorry like.

ROBBIE: As 'e should be.

BOBBO: As 'e should be, that's right. So 'e's like, 'come back to ours, there's more ale and yer can get cleaned up and that.' So I'm havin that, and we get a taxi back to 'is. Pulls up at this big fuck off 'ouse in Blundell Sands.

ROBBIE: Yeah.

BOBBO: So 'e's definitely worth a few bob right.

ROBBIE: I'll say.

BOBBO: So we goes in; it's a palace, and 'e's lappin up everythin I'm sayin, and I know just what to say, just what 'e wants to 'ear. And I'm sittin there thinkin, well I could 'ave 'im off now fer what I can like, or I can barnacle the fucker and 'ave a good ride out of it.

ROBBIE: Barnacle?

BOBBO: Think about it.

ROBBIE: (*Pause.*) I'm on it.

BOBBO: So I tells 'im, me bird'll be worried about me if I don't go 'ome or contact 'er.

ROBBIE: Who's yer bird?

BOBBO: All in good time Robbie.

ROBBIE: Go 'ed.

BOBBO: So I phones 'er back at 'er flat, and I says to James…

ROBBIE: (*Amused.*) James?

BOBBO: I know; 'e doesn't like Jim, or Jimmy fer that matter.

ROBBIE: Sounds like a right tit.

BOBBO: Yeah and I'm milkin 'im like I'm one of dem machines that they attach to cows udders la.

ROBBIE: So yer on the phone to yer tart…

BOBBO: I am and I says to 'im, 'James mate, she doesn't believe me, she thinks I've copped off and she's just not 'avin it.' Right?

ROBBIE: Right.

BOBBO: And I tells 'im that I don't wanna leave 'im in the state 'e's in and that I can't afford to get a taxi 'ome an all that. So 'e says, 'Why don't yer tell 'er to get in a taxi an come up 'ere an I'll pay fer it?' Now that's just what I was waitin fer, 'e was playin right into me 'ands this one.

ROBBIE: You've lost me now mate. What did yer want yer bird there fer?

BOBBO: When I say she's me bird, I mean I'm livin with 'er, I'm shaggin 'er, I'm tuckin into the shoppin, and that's as far as it goes as far as I'm concerned.

ROBBIE: You've barnacled her?

BOBBO: Yer learnin Robbie. So 'e's all for it like and she gets there and we all get talkin fer a bit and then when 'e's avin 'is burst, I tells 'er what I want 'er to do.

ROBBIE: Why what d'yer wann'er to do?

BOBBO: Next thing I'm gonna do is get all tired, 'ave to 'ave a lie down, stop the room from spinnin, all that one.

ROBBIE: Ale gettin to yer?

BOBBO: Was it fuck, I'm a professional me Robbie.

ROBBIE: I'm not with yer.

BOBBO: Yer will be now, because while I'm out the way, it's 'er job to seduce the cunt.

ROBBIE: Yer not a voyeur are yer Bobbo?

BOBBO: I like watchin people fuck, same as the next fellah, but I stayed out the way. Let the bitch get under 'is skin. Anyway, 'e was up fer it, only just; I mean 'e was well gone. But 'is little prick rose to the occasion and 'e 'ad 'er.

ROBBIE: Some mate 'e turned out to be.

BOBBO: Exactly, some mate 'e turned out to be, and when 'e woke up in the mornin and she was in 'is bed and 'is cock stunk of 'er, 'e was well sorry, 'e begged 'er not to tell me, to say that 'e kipped on the couch and all that and give 'er the bed. She was up fer that, as was the plan, and 'e's been me gravy train ever since.

ROBBIE: You've got 'im on a guilt trip?

BOBBO: Got 'im on a guilt trip?

ROBBIE: Yeah.

BOBBO: Not only 'ave I got 'im on a fuckin guilt trip Rob, 'es got a season ticket in first fuckin class.

ROBBIE: Well where will 'e be now.

BOBBO: Scrabblin around lookin fer me.

ROBBIE: Will 'e?

BOBBO: Got 'im into coke. And I'm carrying 'is in case we get pulled.

ROBBIE: Your a 'ead Worker General you la.

BOBBO: Do yer wanna line?

ROBBIE: You've got it 'ere?

BOBBO: Two grammes.

ROBBIE: I dunno, I'm…

BOBBO: (*Finishes sentence for him.*) Gonna get a CD cover to cut it on, that's what.

ROBBIE: We 'aven't got any.

BOBBO: CDs?

ROBBIE: Yeah.

BOBBO: I thought Tina loved music.

ROBBIE: It was 'er life, you know that.

BOBBO: She was somethin special.

ROBBIE: I know.

BOBBO: Should never've 'appened.

ROBBIE: (*Pause.*) What about a record cover?

BOBBO: Go 'ed.

ROBBIE: They're in Wayne's room.

BOBBO: Is 'e in?

ROBBIE: 'E'll be well away.

BOBBO: 'Eavy sleeper?

ROBBIE: 'E is these days, it's that fuckin resin 'e smokes all the time.

BOBBO: Bad gear that lad.

ROBBIE: I know.

BOBBO: Yer wanna get 'im on the skunk.

ROBBIE: I know but it's twenty for an eighth, and 'e can get a half-ounce of resin fer the same price.

BOBBO: Yeah, that's because it's weighed down with all kinds of shite. All the resin that's comin into dis city's full of formaldehyde an shoe polish an Temazepam and fuckin all kinds, not just to make it heavier but to make it more addictive an all.

ROBBIE: Smokin Elvis.

BOBBO: What?

ROBBIE: Mate of mine was in Morocco and 'e got in with some local producer fellahs like and 'e said one night they 'ad this big stack of auld Elvis Presley records right, yer know vinyl? And they was takin them out of the sleeves one by one and droppin an meltin 'em into the resin, you know, in the big vats?

BOBBO: Fuck off!

ROBBIE: Tellin yer.

BOBBO: 'Onest?

ROBBIE: And it was earmarked fer Liverpool.

BOBBO: Fuck that! Smoke it long enough and it'll curl yer lip.

ROBBIE laughs.

Get yer all shook up.

They both find this very funny.

ROBBIE: Puffs 'is face up somethin wicked in the mornin, looks like Mister Potato 'ead.

BOBBO: Doesn't wanna do nothin and all that one.

ROBBIE: That's 'im.

BOBBO: That's resin.

ROBBIE: What can yer do?

BOBBO: Get us that record fer a start.

ROBBIE gets up and leaves the room.

BOBBO pulls a bag from one of his socks and starts to open it.

A few moments later and ROBBIE re-enters carrying a record.

ROBBIE: (*Handing the record to BOBBO.*) Be careful with it.

BOBBO notices something that makes his jaw drop.

BOBBO: (*Pause.*) What am I lookin at 'ere Robbie?

ROBBIE: A record.

BOBBO: Are they real?

ROBBIE: They're real.

BOBBO: John, Paul George and Richard have signed this cover?

ROBBIE: Not long after it was pressed.

BOBBO: It's an original press an all?

ROBBIE: One of the first off it.

BOBBO: Let me get this right, you've got an original signed copy of 'Rubber Soul' by all four Beatles?

ROBBIE: Yer missin one out.

BOBBO: Who, George Best?

ROBBIE: George Best?

BOBBO: He was the fifth fuckin Beatle wan' he?

ROBBIE: No, look.

BOBBO: Oh yeah, is that Epstein's an all?

ROBBIE: We don't go in fer 'alfs 'ere la.

BOBBO: 'Ow did yer get it?

ROBBIE: Keep this to yerself like.

BOBBO: You can trust me Robbie.

ROBBIE: We've got 'em all, all the albums they ever done all signed by them an Epstein, except the ones where 'e was dead.

BOBBO: All originals?

ROBBIE: All originals.

BOBBO: 'Ow?

ROBBIE: They was Tina's.

BOBBO: 'Ow'd she get 'em?

ROBBIE: 'Er Dad was best mates with one of the roadies, and 'e got them for 'er. An all the solo stuff they done, Wings an that. Not just the Fab fuckin Four either. There's all the Mersey Beat bands an all, yer know, Gerry and the Pacemakers an all them lot and then ones Tina got from Frankie Goes to Hollywood and Echo and the Bunnymen, and that from when she was on the scene, giggin an that; all signed by the members, all original, all in first class nick.

BOBBO: I can't cut up on this.

ROBBIE: Why not?

BOBBO: Because it's worth a mint?

ROBBIE: Who to?

BOBBO: You.

ROBBIE: Be careful then.

BOBBO: I will.

BOBBO places the record on his knee and then empties some of the white powder from his bag onto it. He then takes a penknife from his pocket and starts to use it to thin out the coke and farm it into easily snortable lines.

ROBBIE: I 'aven't got any notes fer a tube.

BOBBO: 'S'alright, McDonald's provides.

BOBBO takes a McDonald's straw from his shirt pocket and takes it out of the wrapper and then snips about four inches off it. He discards the longer piece.

'Ere's one I made earlier.

ROBBIE: No yer just made it now.

BOBBO: Oh yeah. Go 'ed.

ROBBIE hesitates.

BOBBO: What are yer waitin fer?

ROBBIE: Which is mine?

BOBBO: Whichever. Just go fer it.

ROBBIE takes the record from BOBBO and is then handed the short straw. He puts it on the couch and leans over it, and then quickly hoovers up one of the generous lines.

ROBBIE: Goal!

BOBBO: Do the other one.

ROBBIE: What about you?

BOBBO: I told yer I've got two grams, thanks to James.

ROBBIE obeys.

BOBBO takes the record back from ROBBIE and starts to sprinkle more coke onto it.

ROBBIE: Feel that!

BOBBO: 'Its yer quick don't it?

ROBBIE: Been awhile.

BOBBO: Yeah?

ROBBIE: You know 'ow it is?

BOBBO: Do I?

ROBBIE: I made some promises; this is a one off.

BOBBO: Promises? Who to?

ROBBIE: Her, me, Wayne…

BOBBO: One offs don't count.

ROBBIE: Course they don't. Nothin counts.

BOBBO: Don't yer reckon?

ROBBIE: Not since they flew them planes into them towers. That was the last time I done a one off.

BOBBO: Yeah?

ROBBIE: Our Wayne 'ad some Es and after I watched the first one go in, I told 'im to go and get them and we dropped three each and just sat there and watched it all 'appen.

BOBBO: You watched all that E'in?

ROBBIE: It was mad.

BOBBO: I bet it was.

ROBBIE: It was. It was… I mean it was so…

BOBBO: What?

ROBBIE: Emotional.

BOBBO: Yeah?

ROBBIE: Oh, all the way. We was sittin there the pair of us on a proper E high, as fellahs in suits jumped out them fuckin windows man.

BOBBO: Fuck.

ROBBIE: Imagine bein in that situation Bobbo.

BOBBO: I know.

ROBBIE: I mean what the fuck does it take to make some fat businessman, jump out one of them winders?

BOBBO: Heat and smoke.

ROBBIE: I sat there with me son, an I'm chewin me tongue off, with me jaw juttin out watchin them wave them white flags at the winders, like they was just sayin 'ello, and I thought that's it.

BOBBO: The world's changed.

ROBBIE: Fuck the world, I'd changed, I mean Tina 'adn't bin gone long, and I was about to get me act together, do some graft, make some dough again.

BOBBO: Yeah?

ROBBIE: And then that 'appens. And I thought fuck that, why should I bother tryin now. It's only a matter of time before they get nukes and then what?

BOBBO: Life goes on.

BOBBO has finished thinning the cocaine and quickly sniffs up two long lines.

ROBBIE: You've got to live fer today now.

BOBBO: I always 'ave.

ROBBIE: More so. Only thing is I'm not even pullin that off.

BOBBO: 'Ow d'yer mean?

ROBBIE: They're stoppin me dole.

BOBBO: (*Outraged.*) What the fuck for?

ROBBIE: 'Ave yer been on New Deal?

BOBBO: Nah, I'm on the sick, 'ave been fer years.

ROBBIE: 'Ow d'yer pull that off?

BOBBO: Irritable Bowel Syndrome.

ROBBIE: Sounds a bit shit.

BOBBO: I wouldn't know, but I've blagged me doctors 'ead that I've got all the symptoms and 'e writes me the ticket.

ROBBIE: I tried to get on with me depression, after Tina died but I didn't score ten out of ten on their little check list.

BOBBO: So what are yer gonna do?

ROBBIE: I dunno, I've got me Auld Fellah and me kid livin 'ere.

BOBBO: Barnacled?

ROBBIE: Barnacled.

BOBBO: You'd get a few bob fer dis record.

ROBBIE: I don't think so.

BOBBO: I'm tellin yer.

ROBBIE: I couldn't.

BOBBO: James buys and sells stuff, antiques an all that.

ROBBIE: Yeah?

BOBBO: (*Indicates record.*) I reckon 'e could get yer a few bob fer this.

ROBBIE: It's not mine to sell.

BOBBO: Whose is it?

ROBBIE: Wayne's.

BOBBO: Leave 'em to 'im did she, in a will?

ROBBIE: She didn't make a will; she wasn't meant to die.

BOBBO: So she never left 'im them, did she?

ROBBIE: Not in that sense.

BOBBO: Not in any sense. Tina died and times got 'ard but she left somethin behind that can get yer on yer feet again, and if you've got as many as yer sayin yer 'ave, then 'e won't notice the odd one's missin.

ROBBIE: 'E's always playin 'em.

BOBBO: So take a couple 'e never plays.

ROBBIE: Nah, no way, e'd lose the plot if 'e found out.

BOBBO: So? Not scared of yer own son are yer Robbie?

ROBBIE: Get a grip. They used to play 'em together.

BOBBO: 'As 'e got a job?

ROBBIE: No.

BOBBO: Is 'e bringin money in?

ROBBIE: No.

BOBBO: Is yer Dad?

ROBBIE: No.

BOBBO: You've been barnacled good and proper 'ere aven't yer?

ROBBIE nods.

So don't yer think you've got the right to make things easier fer yer?

ROBBIE: They was Tina's.

BOBBO: Was.

Pause.

She'd want yer to use 'em to sort things out wouldn't she?

ROBBIE: I dunno.

BOBBO: Course she would. She wouldn't want yer takin some mong's job and losin face, when yer can sell one of these out of so many and feed the fuckin son that she left behind and keep a roof over 'is 'ead. 'E won't notice one.

Pause.

ROBBIE: 'Ave a word with James then; see what 'e says.

BOBBO: No problem.

BOBBO sprinkles more cocaine onto the record cover.

Bet yer glad yer bumped into me.

Music – 'Love in Song' by Wings.

Lights fade to blackout.

Scene 3: The Shrine

Next day around noon. WAYNE's bedroom. It is a shrine to his mother. A blown up framed photograph of her in stage gear hangs on the back wall, with a shelf directly underneath it. On each side of the photograph is a promotional poster for an album by Tina and the Tones. On the shelf are five candles at different stages of burn down. A purple hat with trinkets sewn into it hangs from it on the right. Wayne's bed is directly underneath the shrine, lengthways. Propped against it is an acoustic guitar; it is old and battered and looks to have been repaired with gaffer tape in places. It also has stickers on the front, but they are faded and torn and impossible to decipher. The stage wall has a window and underneath it is an old record player atop a small cupboard. WAYNE is sitting on the corner of the bed staring at the record turning on the music centre. He opens the cupboard doors and runs his fingers along the long row of records that are in there, he selects one and takes it out of the sleeve, he holds it up to the candle light and turns it as the flames flicker on its surface, there is a signature on it in bold black marker ink, which WAYNE copies with his finger (there is something almost religious in the way he does this). He then puts it in the centre of his bedroom floor: it is an album by Tina and the Tones. WAYNE takes a box of matches from his pocket and slowly one after the other lights the five candles. He then takes the hat from the wall and puts it on, before kneeling down and reaching back into the cupboard. He starts to take out more records and lines them up on the floor in a pattern spiralling out from the first record. He stands to look at them, changes the line up, and then changes them again. Tina's record is always central.

WAYNE: What d'yer want?

ROBBIE: Any cups in 'ere?

WAYNE: No.

ROBBIE: Where are they all?

WAYNE: I don't know.

ROBBIE: What are yer doin.

WAYNE: Nothin.

WAYNE starts to put the records back.

ROBBIE: I could've stood on one of them when I came in.

WAYNE: Knock next time.

ROBBIE: D'yer wanna brew?

WAYNE: I'm goin out in a minute.

ROBBIE: Sure the atmosphere won't crush yer.

WAYNE: Funny.

ROBBIE: Where yer goin?

WAYNE: Out.

ROBBIE: Yer gonna see Nan.

WAYNE: No.

ROBBIE notices the tune playing.

ROBBIE: I remember this one.

WAYNE: It was 'er favourite.

ROBBIE: Paul McCartney in'it?

WAYNE: Wings.

ROBBIE: Same difference.

WAYNE: What would you know?

ROBBIE: Which album is it?

WAYNE: What d'you wanna know fer?

ROBBIE: It was 'er favorite wan'it?

WAYNE: 'Venus and Mars'.

ROBBIE: That's the one.

WAYNE: She was there when they signed it.

ROBBIE: That's right.

WAYNE: She said Paul looked tired.

ROBBIE: He looks tired-er now.

WAYNE: Grandad says 'e's a Lizard.

ROBBIE: Who isn't, with 'im?

Pause.

WAYNE takes off the record and puts it back in the sleeve.

WAYNE: There isn't another collection like this in the world.

ROBBIE: Course there will be.

WAYNE: Yeah right.

ROBBIE points to the record in the middle.

ROBBIE: What's that one?

WAYNE: Mum's.

ROBBIE: Oh.

WAYNE picks it up.

WAYNE: I'll never forget the day she came 'ome with it.

ROBBIE: Don't put it on.

WAYNE: Yer think the first thing she'd 'ave done was played it.

ROBBIE: Yeah.

WAYNE: She knew I was diein to 'ear it. But she didn't, she went straight over to the record player and ignored it. She opened the cupboard and she took this and she slid it in amongst them. (*Pause.*) It meant more to 'er that her record was now part of this collection. Every major Liverpool band that 'ad made it and now she was there with them.

ROBBIE: Yeah.

WAYNE: Then she realised something and took it back out and I thought she was goin to put it on at last but she didn't, she took a marker pen out of 'er pocket and she signed it and put it back and said, 'Now it belongs.'

ROBBIE: Yeah.

WAYNE: She left it there fer hours until she put it on.

ROBBIE: It was a good night.

WAYNE: The best.

ROBBIE: Yeah.

WAYNE: Yeah.

WAYNE grabs his guitar and makes his way past his Dad and out of the door and then out of the house.

Music – 'Scared' by John Lennon.

ROBBIE looks at the picture of his wife on the wall. One by one he puts out the candles with his fingers. He puts his fingers to his lips and kisses them then puts his fingers on the lips on the picture. He then turns and kneels down by the record player. He opens the cupboard and looks at the records. He runs his fingers over the spines and then suddenly stops. He selects one of them and looks at it. He shuts the cupboard doors. He is visibly at war with his actions and a little of him seems to die as he sits there looking at the record. Then he stands and leaves the room, heading for the front door, carrying the record with him.

Lights fade to blackout.

Scene 4: Silent Busker

The living room the next day; late afternoon. 'Scared' is still playing. HORSE enters the living room; he is in his boxer shorts, vest and socks that need darning. He looks around the room and stops and looks again. He then starts to rummage under the quilt and cushions, until he finds what he is looking for. It is a pair of grey trousers. He looks at them: they are very creased. He puts them on and continues to search around. He finds an equally creased blue shirt and puts that on. He finds his shoes under the coffee table and puts them on. He then takes them back off and pulls off one of his socks and smells it. He doesn't like the smell and so pulls both off. He looks around some more, but can't find any replacements and so leaves them off and puts his shoes back on. He then heads back over to the bag and wrestles another can from it. Opens it and takes a swig. Then he bends down in front of the back wall couch and feels around underneath it. He pulls out a small plastic bag and sits on the couch looking at it for a moment. Then slowly he pulls out a paperback book, he looks at it and then pulls out another; they are identical. He looks at them both for a moment and then slowly slides them back into the bag and pushes it back under the couch. He then takes off his shirt and shoes and continues to drink his can. The lift rattles into place outside, not long followed by the sound of the front door opening. Music fades. A few moments later and WAYNE enters the living room with his guitar. He is burned from the sun.

WAYNE: Now then.

HORSE: Where've you bin?

WAYNE: Out.

HORSE: Well I can see that. I thought vampires couldn't go out in the day.

WAYNE: Funny.

HORSE: Then again by the looks of yer any longer out there and yer probably would've started smokin.

WAYNE: I'm not in the mood Grandad.

HORSE: Cows have moods lad, cows and women.

HORSE grabs a small battery operated fan from the mess on the coffee table and switches it on; fanning his face.

WAYNE: Is me Dad in?

HORSE: Nope. (*Beat.*) Yer burnt yer know?

WAYNE: I know.

HORSE: Badly.

WAYNE: I've never known it be so 'ot.

WAYNE goes to the kitchen and pours himself a drink.

HORSE: Little present from the women of the world.

WAYNE: Yer what?

HORSE: This 'eat.

WAYNE: I'm not on yer.

HORSE: All that fuckin 'airspray an shite they've bin sprayin all over 'em selves.

WAYNE: What about it.

HORSE: It's like that creature's blood in the *Alien* film. Yer know the bit where they slice through one of the fingers when it's wrapped round 'is neck and its blood spurts out and splashes on the floor and keeps goin through each deck of the ship like some sort of super acid. Same thing see, only their 'airspray shite goes up instead of down, and it's eatin big chunks out the sky.

WAYNE comes back in.

WAYNE: So are they all Lizards as well?

HORSE: Who?

WAYNE: Women.

HORSE: Not all of 'em.

WAYNE: What about Nan?

HORSE: She never used 'airspray, not ever. Bad fer 'er chest see. Still 'ad a lovely smell in 'er 'air though.

WAYNE: Hasn't she now?

HORSE: Yer know we always read the same book at the same time don't yer?

WAYNE: 'Ow?

HORSE: We'd buy two copies of the same book, make up a big flask of Ovaltine or Horlicks and we'd sit in the bed with a bit of Billie Holliday in the background, just on nice and low, yer know and we'd read, at the same speed, turn the papers at the same time, laugh at the same jokes on the page, then have a chin wag about the chapter we'd just read together, yer know. We'd be leaning in close and I'd be able to smell 'er 'air and I still don't know why it smelled so good, see'n as she didn't mess around with spray.

WAYNE: Yer can still ask 'er.

HORSE: We never finished the last book.

WAYNE: What was it?

HORSE: (*Pause.*) Yer need some cream on yer skin.

WAYNE: Like we're gonna 'ave some cream 'ere.

HORSE: Yer can get sick, gettin burnt like that.

WAYNE: I feel sick.

HORSE: Where've yer bin?

WAYNE: Town.

HORSE: Town, you?

WAYNE: What's the big deal?

HORSE: 'Ow did yer scrape yerself away from yer bucket?

WAYNE: I've ran out of weed.

HORSE: That doesn't usually stop yer. Yer scrape all that brown gooey gunk from the inside of yer bottle and smoke it all over again don't yer?

WAYNE: It's oil.

HORSE: Tar more like. (*Real distaste.*) Sediment. Pluh!

WAYNE: It gets yer stoned.

HORSE: Then when that's all gone yer starts crawlin round

the floor combin the bleedin carpet fer little grains of pot.

WAYNE: Only when there's a drought on.

HORSE: I've seen yer put any little brown crumb yer find in that thing.

WAYNE: Listen to Hawkeye there.

HORSE: You've probably smoked auld dried up baked beans and bogeys and all kinds in that thing.

WAYNE: Yeah well not this time.

HORSE: No I can see.

WAYNE: I just wish…

HORSE: What lad?

WAYNE: I couldn't do it.

HORSE: Do what?

WAYNE: Yer see other people doin it, just sittin off and singin some Oasis shite that even they couldn't make sound alright.

HORSE: 'Ave yer bin buskin?

WAYNE: Sort of.

HORSE: Sort of what?

WAYNE: It just wouldn't come out.

HORSE: What wouldn't?

WAYNE: Me voice. (*Pause.*) Every time I opened me mouth to sing it came out small. Like it wasn't even mine; like there was some tiny little fellah this big, (*Shows a couple centimeters with his finger and thumb.*) sat at the back of me throat and he was doin the singin.

HORSE: Probably just as well, yer don't want people suin yer fer breach of the peace.

WAYNE: I just wanted to make us some money Grandad.

HORSE: Good on yer kid but I'm not sure that's the way to do it.

WAYNE: Me Mam did.

HORSE: Not enough fer yers to live on.

WAYNE: I'm not losing this flat. See that? (*Points to something on the wall.*) That's one of 'er 'airs.

HORSE: What is?

WAYNE: There, an 'air from 'er 'ead.

HORSE: Where?

WAYNE: She must 'ave brushed against the wall one time and it got caught in a little nick in the wallpaper.

HORSE: It could be anyone's that kid.

WAYNE: It's me Mum's, right down to its split end and grey root. She's all over this flat, I can smell 'er like you can smell Nan's 'air, and I'm not losin it, cos yer can't take things like that with yer can yer?

HORSE: No.

WAYNE: So if you won't work and Dad won't work then I'll 'ave to.

HORSE: Did yer make anythin then?

WAYNE: Not a button.

HORSE: Yer should of sat in the shade.

WAYNE: I did.

HORSE: 'Ow comes yer so burnt then?

WAYNE: Because I only had enough money to get the bus one-way, and like a nob 'ead, I thought I'd make at least enough to get back the same way. But seen as the bus driver don't accept invisible buttons I 'ad to walk it.

HORSE: In this 'eat?

WAYNE: I know, I feel like shit.

HORSE: Yer look like Admiral Akkabar.

WAYNE: Who?

HORSE: Lobster fellah from *Return of the Jedi*.

WAYNE: I've never seen it.

HORSE: Yer 'aven't seen the *Star Wars* Trilogy?

WAYNE: Load of bollocks all that in'it?

HORSE: Wash yer shitty mouth out. Yer don't know what yer missin kid. Works of art them films. Me and yer Nan took yer Dad to see all of 'em. He 'ad all the little men.

WAYNE: They're worth money them.

HORSE: Not after 'e'd 'ad 'em. 'E used to stand 'em up in dog shite and say they was caught in quick sand.

WAYNE: Uuurgh!

HORSE: Runnier the better.

WAYNE: I don't wanna know.

HORSE: Imagine drownin in shit.

WAYNE: I feel like I am.

HORSE: *Empire Strikes Back* was the best.

WAYNE: 'E told me 'e never played with toys.

HORSE: 'E's right; 'e tortured them instead. Great films, great films. The new ones are all me arse though. Lizards got to Lucas in the end; sucked 'is brains out through his nostrils with their little pipettes, or whatever it is they do.

They sit in silence for a moment and then WAYNE, feeling utterly defeated, pulls his bottle out of the bucket and turns it in the light as the water drips from it. There is a thick brown tar darker at the neck but covering the inside of half of the bottle. WAYNE gets up and goes into the kitchen and looks for something in the draws.

WAYNE: (*Through the hatch.*) Where's all the knifes?

HORSE: What?

WAYNE: The knives?

HORSE: Any eggs?

WAYNE: No!

WAYNE re-enters holding a spoon. He goes back to his bucket and starts to scrape the tar from the inside of his bottle.

HORSE: (*Sings.*) 'Scooby Dooby Doo, where are you? I've got some work for you now. Dee dee dee dee dum dah dum dee dee dah doo dah doo dah doo dah!'

WAYNE: (*Amused.*) Stop smokin crack.

HORSE: I love that show.

WAYNE: *Scooby Doo?*

HORSE: (*Impression.*) 'Scooby Dooby Doo!!!!!!'

WAYNE: It's a cartoon.

HORSE: Is it?

WAYNE: Yeah.

HORSE: Get out of it.

WAYNE: I'm tellin yer.

HORSE: Think I'm too auld fer cartoons do yer kid?

WAYNE: Just a bit like.

HORSE: Me an Alice loved watchin cartoons with the kids and we just carried on when they left.

WAYNE: Yer jokin?

HORSE: Especially *Scooby Doo.*

WAYNE: Why?

HORSE: It's a mystery in'it? We liked to try and work out who the baddy was.

WAYNE: There's only ever two fellahs it could be.

HORSE: That's why we liked it, yer get it right fifty percent of the time.

WAYNE: 'Ave yer seen the film?

HORSE: Don't mention it; sacrilege!

WAYNE: Looks alright to me, Scooby's a bit shit though.

HORSE: The Lizards 'ave made it, tryin to corrupt the cartoons, see?

WAYNE: I'm sick of 'earing about yer stupid fuckin Lizards.

HORSE: There's nothin stupid about 'em kid, so don't make the mistake of thinkin so.

WAYNE: If yer say so.

HORSE: I say so.

WAYNE: And what are they supposed to be up to anyway.

HORSE: We're not sure where they're from.

WAYNE: Who isn't?

HORSE: People who are onto 'em, like David Icke an me.

WAYNE: Never 'eard of him.

HORSE: Surprise, surprise, when they control the media. Yer see kid, wherever they're from, whether it be hell or space or some other fuckin dimension, they're 'ere see, and that's that. Twelve foot fuckin Lizards that have taken on human form and gotten themselves into positions of power all over the world. Bush is one, Blair's one, Wacko Jacko's one and so's that Anthony Worrel Thomkinson. And what they're doin is, they're shapin the world to suit themselves see? Orchestratin things like the war in Iraq and September 11th.

WAYNE: What the fuck for?

HORSE: (*Embarrassed at not actually knowing.*) That's the big fuckin question isn't it? (*Beat.*) What ever it is it's not good.

Pause.

WAYNE: Bollocks.

HORSE: Yer what?

WAYNE: Bollocks.

HORSE: I'm tellin yer.

WAYNE: Stop smoking crack.

HORSE: Watch yer back kid.

Noise off stage of lift rattling into place.

WAYNE: Does Nan believe in these Lizards an all?

HORSE goes to say something but stops. Sound of the front door being opened. Then ROBBIE strides into the room. He has lots of shopping bags. He is blissfully drunk.

ROBBIE: Now then boys, Daddy's 'ome.

HORSE: What 'ave yer got there?

ROBBIE: What I've got 'ere is the fruit of my labours.

HORSE: Oh I?

ROBBIE: Plenty of scran.

ROBBIE starts throwing food at them to catch. Biscuits and cakes and other junk.

Beer fer me an you Pops, and I've even got yer a weed Wayne.

ROBBIE shows and then throws a chunk of resin to WAYNE.

WAYNE: Nice one Dad.

ROBBIE: Don't fuckin mention it kid. If I can't feed me kid an get 'im stoned, what kind of a Dad am I? And get on this.

WAYNE: What?

ROBBIE pulls a small white packet out of his back pocket and holds them up.

ROBBIE: Not one, but six new strings fer yer guit.

WAYNE: Yes!

ROBBIE: 'Ang on, 'ang on la, and some plecks.

ROBBIE throws the strings at WAYNE followed by a bunch of plectrums, all different colours and thickness. They rain on a happy WAYNE.

WAYNE: Is right Dad.

ROBBIE: Is right Son.

WAYNE: Look at these Grandad.

HORSE: Mmmm.

ROBBIE: Best strings an all.

WAYNE: 'Ave yer got some work?

ROBBIE staggers closer, the bags swinging round.

ROBBIE: Wayne, Wayne, Wayne, Wayne, don't yer trust me lad?

WAYNE: Yeah.

ROBBIE is in WAYNE's face now.

ROBBIE: No look, look I'm askin yer a question 'ere right.

WAYNE: I know.

ROBBIE: Don't yer trust me?

WAYNE: Course I do.

ROBBIE: Course 'e does. Dad? See, course 'e does. What! No worries, I've struck gold and I'm sortin things out, and it's all gonna be hunky fuckin dory.

WAYNE stops his scraping and starts to build a proper bucket.

WAYNE: Yer want one Dad?

ROBBIE: No, I'm laughin, I've got all these beers.

HORSE: 'Ave we won the lottery.

ROBBIE: I like the way yer get the 'we' in there Dad. No, 'we' 'aven't won the lottery; I put a bet on.

HORSE: You don't bet.

ROBBIE: Well I fuckin do now, and I won.

HORSE: 'Ow much?

ROBBIE: Seven hundred smack-a-fuckin-roonies.

WAYNE: Is right Dad.

ROBBIE: I told yers I'd sort it out.

HORSE: Fer now yer 'ave. What about when you've ran out of that?

ROBBIE: I'll put another bet on.

HORSE: Think yer gonna win every time d'yer?

ROBBIE: I've got a good tipper.

HORSE: Get real Robbie.

ROBBIE: Yer should of seen everyone in the Jaw Bone, when I bought a round in. Robbie Boil is back on the scene.

HORSE: Been buyin crap?

ROBBIE: What's up Horse, feeling left out? Now then, me little Barnacle's got his weed and his strings and that. (*He looks at his Dad.*) I wonder what I've got in me bag fer me big Barnacle.

ROBBIE looks in one of his bags and looks back at HORSE with a big grin.

HORSE: What is it?

ROBBIE draws closer to HORSE.

ROBBIE: A lizard.

ROBBIE whips out a stuffed lizard from his bag and shoves it in front of his Dad's face. HORSE recoils in shock.

HORSE: Get it away from me!

ROBBIE: (*Confused.*) What?

HORSE: Get it away!

ROBBIE: It's stuffed.

HORSE: Please…

ROBBIE: Cost a bomb that.

WAYNE: 'Ere are dad.

ROBBIE: It's not alive.

WAYNE: Get it away from 'im.

ROBBIE: What's up with yers?

HORSE is in terror.

WAYNE: Look at him.

ROBBIE: (*Waving it in HORSE's face.*) It's dead yer fuckin fruit.

WAYNE gets up and grabs the lizard.

WAYNE: Give it 'ere.

ROBBIE: Get off it.

WAYNE: Give it us.

ROBBIE: Yer rippin it!

WAYNE: Just let go…

WAYNE pulls it away and takes it over to the window and throws the stuffed lizard out of it.

ROBBIE: What did yer go and do that for?

WAYNE: 'E was terrified of it.

ROBBIE: No 'e wasn't.

WAYNE: 'E was.

ROBBIE: Was yer Dad?

WAYNE: Leave 'im.

ROBBIE: I thought 'e'd like it.

HORSE: You can't make me go and see her! D'yer 'ear me.

ROBBIE: What?

HORSE: I can't face 'er eyes. So yer can't make me, see! You or any bastard fuckin lizard.

HORSE storms out of the room.

ROBBIE looks at WAYNE and then sits down.

ROBBIE: I thought 'e'd like it.

Music – 'Happiness is a Warm Gun' by the Beatles.

Lights fade to blackout

Scene 5: Storm in a tea bowl

The Living Room, midday, two days later. WAYNE and BOBBO enter the living room from the front door. They are both drenched.

BOBBO: Fuckin 'ell la, where'd that come from?

WAYNE: I know.

BOBBO: Made up you come along there. Bastard wouldn't let us in.

WAYNE: Who security?

BOBBO: Yeah.

WAYNE: Dickheads mate. Little Hitlers me Dad calls 'em. They won't even let us in if we forget our fob. They know we live 'ere like but they pretend that they don't.

BOBBO: Do me 'ead in that. (*Pause.*) Where is 'e anyway?

WAYNE: Me Dad?

BOBBO: Supposed to be meetin me 'ere about 'alf an hour ago.

WAYNE: Fuck knows.

BOBBO: Proper soaked now la.

WAYNE: 'E should be 'ere soon.

BOBBO: 'Ave yer got a towel or somethin?

WAYNE has a look around the room. He exits into the hall and goes into the bathroom. He comes back with a towel and throws it at BOBBO. It is discoloured and stained and soaking wet.

It's wetter than me that kidda. Did yer get it of the bathroom floor?

WAYNE: S'all there is.

BOBBO: (*Sniffing it.*) Smells like an auld man. (*Pause.*) What's that? (*He points to a sweatshirt hanging over the arm of one of the couches.*)

WAYNE: Sweatshirt.

BOBBO: Is it clean?

WAYNE: Why?

BOBBO picks it up and smells it.

BOBBO: Bit ripe, but it'll 'ave to do.

BOBBO uses the sweatshirt to dry himself.

WAYNE: Was yer out with me Dad the other night?

BOBBO: Yeah.

WAYNE: Yers 'aven't seen each other in ages 'ave yer?

BOBBO: Not fer a while.

WAYNE: 'E doesn't go out.

BOBBO: 'E does now.

WAYNE: 'Ow d'yer mean?

BOBBO: 'E's got a taste fer it again now 'asn't 'e? (*Pause.*) Do us a brew?

WAYNE: What are yer meetin 'im 'ere for?

BOBBO: Bit of business.

WAYNE: Business?

BOBBO: Four sugars.

WAYNE: What?

BOBBO: In me tea.

WAYNE heads into the kitchen and puts the kettle on.

BOBBO goes over to the window and looks out.

WAYNE: 'Ave you been givin 'im 'is tips?

BOBBO: Tips?

WAYNE: For the 'orses?

BOBBO: Yer could say that. (*Pause.*) D'yer still knock round with our Barry and that?

WAYNE: Nah.

BOBBO: I thought you's were best mates?

WAYNE: 'Ow many sugars again?

BOBBO: Four. (*Pause.*) Who d'yer knock round with now den?

WAYNE: No one.

BOBBO: No one? (*Pause.*) 'Ow come?

WAYNE: Couldn't be arsed.

BOBBO: Couldn't be arsed 'angin around with yer best mates?

WAYNE: D'yer want milk?

BOBBO: Loads. (*Pause.*) You wanna get yer Dad to redecorate this place.

WAYNE re-enters carrying two bowls of tea.

WAYNE: We like it the way it is. 'Ere.

BOBBO: What the fuck's that?

WAYNE: All the cups are broke.

BOBBO takes the bowl of tea.

BOBBO: Tellin yer Wayney boy, either of yers bring any birds back 'ere and they'd soon be off.

WAYNE: We don't want no birds round 'ere.

BOBBO: Why not?

WAYNE: Mam wouldn't like it.

Pause.

BOBBO: Got any draw?

WAYNE: Might 'ave.

BOBBO: Pass it 'ere then and I'll build a joint.

WAYNE goes over to the TV and picks his lump of resin off the top. He tosses it to BOBBO.

BOBBO pulls out some skins and tobacco and begins building a joint.

WAYNE sits next to him and builds a bucket.

Smells like petrol.

WAYNE: Don't smoke it then.

BOBBO continues to build.

D'yer wanna 'ear some sounds?

BOBBO: Got any Nick Drake?

WAYNE: Is 'e from Liverpool?

BOBBO: No.

WAYNE: Then we 'aven't got 'im.

BOBBO: Yer missin out la, proper stoner music it is. Mellow as fuck.

WAYNE: What about about a bit of McCartney?

BOBBO: What about – I'd rather listen to me own Grandma being fuckin tortured by Bin Laden and 'is merry men.

WAYNE: 'E's the best.

BOBBO: Lennon was the best.

WAYNE: Name yer three favorite Beatle songs.

BOBBO: Why?

WAYNE: Come on.

BOBBO: 'Long and Windin Road', 'Hey Jude' and er 'For No One'.

WAYNE: They're all McCartney ones. Lennon didn't even 'ave an 'and in 'em. Apart from one measly line in 'Hey Jude', and alls that was that he told Paul to leave a line in that he was gonna take out.

BOBBO: 'Ow d'you know.

WAYNE: 'Cos I'm a fuckin expert.

BOBBO: Lennon was cooler.

WAYNE: 'E beat 'is wife; 'ow cool's that?

BOBBO: Lennon 'ad it 'ard.

WAYNE: 'Aven't we all.

BOBBO: Bit of a know it all aren't yer?

WAYNE: I love Lennon like, I just think Macca 'as the edge, the melodies yer know, they speak to the soul.

BOBBO: I sold my soul a long time ago. (*Pause.*) 'Ave yer got all 'is records.

WAYNE: Course.

BOBBO: Which d'yer play the most?

WAYNE: 'Venus and Mars'.

BOBBO: Why that one?

WAYNE: It was me Mam's favourite.

BOBBO: What about 'er record?

WAYNE: What about it?

BOBBO: D'yer ever play it?

WAYNE: Only when me Dad's not in.

BOBBO: 'E never did like 'er music did 'e?

WAYNE: What does 'e know?

BOBBO: They was a bit like 'Venus and Mars'.

WAYNE: Me Mam an Dad?

BOBBO: Talk about opposites.

WAYNE: Suppose.

BOBBO: She could've 'ad anyone back in the day like.

WAYNE: Yer reckon?

BOBBO: Everyone 'ad a crush on Tina.

WAYNE: Yeah?

BOBBO: Oh yeah. Jammy bastard your Dad.

WAYNE: 'E's not now.

BOBBO: You never saw 'er play live with 'er band did yer?

WAYNE: She played to me in me room.

BOBBO: But yer never saw 'er on stage?

WAYNE: No.

BOBBO: She was amazin. Those songs that voice, and them costumes la. You missed a treat.

WAYNE: Me Dad wouldn't take me.

BOBBO: Sad.

WAYNE: I wanted to go but 'e said I was to young.

BOBBO: Or 'e just couldn't bear to listen to 'er songs.

WAYNE: What was she like?

BOBBO: Yer 'ad to be there.

WAYNE: Come on tell us.

BOBBO: Got any biscuits?

WAYNE: Yeah.

BOBBO: Get us some then.

> *WAYNE heads to the kitchen.*

> When she came on she 'ad the crowd in 'er palm, straight off the bat. She should have been a big star.

> *WAYNE returns with the biscuits and hands them to BOBBO.*

> But yer know if yer 'aven't got the… (*Trails off.*)

WAYNE: The what?

BOBBO: Nothin.

WAYNE: No go on.

BOBBO: Nah I can't say.

WAYNE: 'Aven't got the what Bobbo?

BOBBO: I'm not dissin me best mate like.

WAYNE: Me Dad?

BOBBO: 'E didn't support 'er did 'e? (*Pause.*) When 'er record bombed. 'E was always telling 'er to give up, and then when that 'appened with the album… 'e didn't exactly try and pick up the pieces did 'e?

WAYNE: No.

BOBBO: Not 'is fault like, she was from Venus and 'e was from fuckin Pluto.

WAYNE: I tried.

BOBBO: Course yer did kidda, you was 'er number one fan, everyone knows that.

WAYNE: I couldn't' get through.

BOBBO: You was just a kid, things'd be different now.

WAYNE: I tried to tell 'er she still 'ad me.

BOBBO: That was yer Dad's job, not a kid's.

Pause.

Let's see it?

WAYNE: What?

BOBBO: 'Er record.

WAYNE: Come in me room.

WAYNE and BOBBO enter the bedroom.

BOBBO sees the blown up photo of Tina and the shrine and jumps.

BOBBO: Jesus, thought someone was in 'ere then.

WAYNE goes to the record cupboard and finds Tina's record. He shows it to BOBBO.

BOBBO continues to look at the picture.

Put it on.

WAYNE takes the album out of its cover and places it on the deck, he is just about to put the needle in place, when the sound of the lift rattles into place.

WAYNE: That'll be me Dad. I can't play it now.

BOBBO: I'll 'ear it another time then. Anyway, 'bout fuckin time 'e showed up, busy man me yer know.

WAYNE: Yer always was.

BOBBO: And always will be Wayney boy. (*Pats WAYNE's head.*) Always will be.

WAYNE: Get off.

The front door opens and ROBBIE walks through the hall and spots WAYNE and BOBBO in the bedroom. He is also very wet.

BOBBO: Where've you bin?

ROBBIE: Just 'avin a walk. What are yers doin in 'ere?

BOBBO: In that rain?

ROBBIE: Refreshin, yer know. What's goin on?

BOBBO: Refreshin? It nearly broke me back it come down that 'ard. Wayne let us in while I was waitin.

ROBBIE: What are yers doin in 'ere?

WAYNE: Isn't Grandad with yer?

ROBBIE: No.

WAYNE: 'E 'asn't been in all mornin.

BOBBO: I thought we 'ad some business to do la?

ROBBIE: (*Awkward.*) We do.

BOBBO: James is waitin.

ROBBIE: E's gonna 'ave to wait then isn't he?

BOBBO: I don't know about that, time's money to 'im an all that. 'E's only doin it fer yer fer a favour, 'cos yer me best mate; it's not like 'e's makin anything out of it.

WAYNE: Out of what?

ROBBIE: Wayne, can yer do me a big favour?

WAYNE: What now?

ROBBIE: I forgot to get me cans.

WAYNE: What's that got to do with me?

ROBBIE: Will yer go and get me some.

WAYNE: I've just got in.

ROBBIE: I'll get yer another weed.

WAYNE: I'm wet.

ROBBIE: The sun's back out now, it'll dry yer off.

WAYNE: I'll get 'em later.

ROBBIE: I want 'em now.

WAYNE: Fuckin 'ell.

WAYNE gets up and puts his hand out towards his Dad. ROBBIE hands WAYNE a ten-pound note.

ROBBIE: Get us eight cans of Stella and spend the rest on sweets or whatever.

WAYNE puts the record sleeve on the bed and leaves.

BOBBO: Get the goods then.

ROBBIE: I dunno Bobbo.

BOBBO: I thought we'd bin through this.

ROBBIE: I mean I'm alright fer now aren't I?

BOBBO: 'E's got this feller all the way up from London la,

81

big collector.

ROBBIE: I know but…

BOBBO: He only wants three. They 'ave to be these three.

BOBBO hands ROBBIE a piece of paper.

You'll get a grand Robbie.

ROBBIE: A grand?

BOBBO: Come on, Robbie Boil's back on the scene in'e?

ROBBIE: Yeah.

BOBBO: Everyone's bin sayin 'ow made up they are to see yer propin up a bar again.

ROBBIE: Yeah?

BOBBO: I'm tellin yer. Talk of the town you la.

ROBBIE: Lets 'ave a look then.

ROBBIE leans down in front of the music cupboard and opens it. He finds the appropriate records and takes them out one by one. He turns and hands them to BOBBO.

ROBBIE: Yer better get goin, before Wayne gets back.

BOBBO: I'll be in the JB at about six with the spondoolies.

ROBBIE nods and BOBBO takes one last look at the picture of Tina and quickly leaves. ROBBIE notices Tina's album cover on the bed and picks it up. He notices the record is not in it and looks at the turntable. Slowly he puts the needle into position and the first track begins to play. The haunting notes of a piano fill the room, followed by Tina's voice.

TINA'S VOICE: (*Recorded.*) 'The World it has no pain, it has no brain, it is a drain for human thoughts. Life shall meet death, in one final breath; it's just the way that all things are. The World it has…'

During this ROBBIE breaks down: he can't handle it and

he stands and knocks the needle off the record with a scratch, and leans over the player, sobbing. Blackout.

End of Act One.

ACT TWO

Scene 1: Songsmith

Liverpool City Centre, the next day. Downstage centre, WAYNE is perched on a step, with his guitar on his lap. He has a small cloth sack at his feet. He has just started the opening chords of one of his own compositions ('Broken Heart'), then he sings, his voice is weak at first, but gets stronger, and grows in confidence as the song progresses. There is a terrible sadness conveyed in the emotion of the singing and weariness beyond the young man's years. He is wearing his mother's hat.

WAYNE: (*Singing.*)
Broken heart, broken heart, broken heart, she broke
my heart.
I've been in this city for ten thousand years and I don't
seem to be able to find my way out.
I'd been sitting pretty with a girlfriend of mine and I
didn't seem to notice, she'd found her way out.
I don't believe in Milk and Cream, I don't believe in
love it seems,
I don't believe in broken dreams,
no I don't believe in these.
I've been in big trouble with sex crazy doctors and I
didn't seem to be able, to find my way out.
So I gave them some candy in brown paper bags, but
they didn't seem able, to get anything out.
I don't believe in ice in drinks, I don't believe in hate
me thinks,
I don't believe in bends and kinks,
no I don't believe in these, these, these, please.
Broken heart, broken heart, broken heart, she broke my
heart.
I met a small group of strange cattle killers, who it
seems to me where all pretty fucked up.
So I drank Indian tea in a white china cup, with a young
Jamaican who said, 'Hey Mon I've given it up.'

I don't believe in wishful thinking, don't believe under drinking,
don't believe in quiet tinkering,
no I don't believe in these,
I don't believe in ups and downs, don't believe in hidden frowns,
I don't believe in ghost towns,
no I don't believe in these,
I don't believe in triangles,
don't believe in Jesus sandals, don't believe in no fallen angels,
no I don't believe in these, these, these, please.
Broken heart, broken heart, broken heart, she broke my heart.
So look at me like an open book and I'll try to keep quite still,
but don't you mess with my soul.
Yeah look at me like an open book and I'll try to keep quite still,
but don't you mess with my soul.

WAYNE stops playing.

The lights fade to blackout.

Scene 2: Bad Company

Music – 'Running Away' by Tina and the Tones.

WAYNE's bedroom. Late afternoon. ROBBIE is leaning in front of the record cupboard searching for more records. The buzzer has just been answered by HORSE near the front door. ROBBIE takes out four records and places them in a suitcase near his side. HORSE hears the case snap shut in WAYNE'S room and looks in. This makes ROBBIE jump.

Music ends.

HORSE: What are yer doin in 'ere Son?

ROBBIE: Talkin to T.

HORSE: Oh sorry.

ROBBIE: 'S'alright.

HORSE: Everythin okay?

ROBBIE: This fuckin 'eat's doin me 'ead in!

HORSE: Tell me about it. It's like bein in the fuckin tropics.

ROBBIE: 'Ow would you know? You've never been out of the country.

HORSE: I've bin to Wales arse wipe.

ROBBIE: Ooh, last of the great wanderers.

HORSE: Yer know what it is, they're changing the climate to suit themselves, see?

ROBBIE: Who is?

HORSE: Who d'yer think?

ROBBIE: It's too hot fer this.

HORSE: The Lizards that's who.

ROBBIE: Jesus!

HORSE: They're doin it through the women, just like I told are Wayne. Cold blood see?

ROBBIE: It's you who've lost yer marbles not me Mam.

HORSE: What?

ROBBIE: Nothin, sorry. (*Pause.*) What d'yer want anyway?

HORSE: The buzzer's just gone.

ROBBIE: Did yer answer it?

HORSE: Yeah, it's someone fer you.

ROBBIE: Bobbo?

HORSE: Sounded somethin like that.

ROBBIE: It'll be Bobbo. Did yer buzz 'im in?

HORSE: Not the same Bobbo from years back?

ROBBIE: Is he comin up?

HORSE: Kelly Morgan's kid.

ROBBIE: That's 'im.

HORSE: What the fuck does 'e want 'ere.

ROBBIE: To see me, what d'yer think?

HORSE: 'E's not comin in 'ere.

ROBBIE: What Wayne's room?

HORSE: This flat, 'e's not fuckin comin into this flat.

ROBBIE: Says who?

HORSE: Says me.

ROBBIE: Says you?

HORSE: That's what I said.

ROBBIE: Stop smokin crack Dad.

HORSE: I don't want 'im in me 'ome.

ROBBIE: This isn't your 'ome.

HORSE: 'E's one nasty piece of work that lad.

ROBBIE: Bobbo?

HORSE: No Rupert the fuckin Bear, that's who.

ROBBIE: Get off yer crack pipe.

HORSE: I wouldn't know what a crack pipe was if yer shoved one up me crack lad, but I know some around 'ere who must be cracked to let 'im in.

ROBBIE: Look if yer wanna keep livin 'ere yer can't go shoutin the odds on who comes in and who doesn't.

HORSE: When 'e comes to the door I want you to tell 'im to sling it.

ROBBIE: Why what the fuck's wrong with 'im?

HORSE: What's wrong with 'im? What's right with him, more like?

ROBBIE: 'E's alright.

HORSE: No 'e's not alright.

ROBBIE: What 'ave yer 'eard?

HORSE: 'Part from the fact that everyone 'ates 'im, I've 'eard rumours.

ROBBIE: What rumours?

HORSE: I 'eard 'e done some time fer blaggin auld people out of there money.

ROBBIE: Is that it?

HORSE: 'E'd knock on their doors and pretend to be from the church or the gas or what have yer and while they're makin 'im a cup of tea, 'e'd 'ave 'em off.

ROBBIE: 'E wouldn't do that now.

HORSE: What if 'e done other things?

ROBBIE: What other things?

HORSE seems to shrivel a little.

Just behave.

There is a knock on the front door from off stage. Quickly followed by a shout through the letterbox.

BOBBO: (*From off stage.*) Robbie.

HORSE: Don't let 'im in.

BOBBO: (*From off stage.*) Robbie.

ROBBIE: 'Old on. Just cool it Dad.

They stare at each other for a second and then ROBBIE heads for the bedroom door followed by HORSE who goes into the living room as ROBBIE makes for the front door. He opens it and BOBBO follows him into the living room.

BOBBO: Ride to the door on a snail did yer? (*On entering and seeing the old man.*) Now then Horse, long time no see, 'ow's it goin kidder?

HORSE: Lot worse all of a sudden.

BOBBO: What's up with yer? Prostrate playin yer up?

HORSE is unsettled by BOBBO's presence.

HORSE: Think yer funny lad?

BOBBO: I 'ave me moments.

ROBBIE: Does 'e want more?

BOBBO: Who?

ROBBIE: Who d'yer think?

BOBBO: Oh 'e wants more alright.

ROBBIE: Yeah?

BOBBO: 'E said keep them records comin.

ROBBIE: That simple?

BOBBO: That simple.

HORSE: What records?

ROBBIE: Nothin fer yer to worry yer swiss cheese over.

HORSE: I'll be the judge of that.

BOBBO: 'E's funny 'im la.

HORSE: Somethin to laugh at because I'm auld yer mean.

BOBBO: Been on the scrumpy again Grandad?

HORSE: Is that what we are to you, some sort of sick entertainment?

BOBBO: What's 'e on about.

ROBBIE: Dad what the fuck are yer on about now.

HORSE: I'm just sayin…

ROBBIE: Well give it a rest.

BOBBO: Chill out and that.

ROBBIE: Sooner yer get the cash fer them Bobbo, sooner I can take me and you on the bender of a lifetime.

BOBBO: Lovely.

HORSE: What's goin on 'ere?

BOBBO: 'Aven't yer got some medicine to take or somethin Pops?

HORSE: Are you goin to let 'im talk to me like that Robert?

ROBBIE: Just cool it Dad.

ROBBIE goes into the kitchen.

HORSE and BOBBO continue to talk in hushed tones.

HORSE: Visited any old people lately.

BOBBO: Not fer a while.

HORSE: So it's true then?

BOBBO: What is?

HORSE: Yer like rippin old people off.

BOBBO: Auld, young, somewhere in the middle, didn't matter to me.

HORSE: Scum.

BOBBO: Loser.

HORSE: What?

BOBBO: What's up Pops, 'fraid someone round 'ere's gonna make somethin of 'emselves?

HORSE: What, with your 'elp?

BOBBO: You've got me all wrong mate; You've been listenin to idle chit-chat. Talkin to too many auld bags at the bus stop.

HORSE: Mess with us kid and you'll regret it.

BOBBO: Why what are yer gonna do? Everyone knows you've lost it.

HORSE shrivels.

BOBBO: Yer didn't retire; yer ran away like a girl.

ROBBIE re-enters carrying three cans hanging from the plastic four-pack holder from his teeth.

ROBBIE: You two gettin on?

BOBBO: Like two shaved bears in a barrel of bees mate.

ROBBIE hands BOBBO his can and then HORSE his, before opening and taking a sip of his own.

BOBBO: Still into all yer conspiracy theories Horse?

ROBBIE: More than ever.

HORSE: They aren't theories, they're facts.

BOBBO: Dropped too much acid in the sixties you.

HORSE: Think yer fuckin smart don't yer?

BOBBO: Do I?

HORSE: Think yer know it all, but yer don't, both of yers know nothin.

BOBBO: Is that right.

HORSE: When yer go into these auld people houses what d'yer take?

BOBBO: I don't do that no more, that was a bad patch that.

HORSE: What did yer take then?

ROBBIE: Wind yer neck in there Dad.

BOBBO: Whatever I could make money out of.

HORSE: What else did yer take?

BOBBO: What else is there?

Pause.

ROBBIE pulls a ten-pound note from his pocket.

ROBBIE: 'Ere, if I give yer a tenner will you go to the flicks?

HORSE: Piss off.

ROBBIE: Fuckin go and see Nan then.

BOBBO: Why where is she?

HORSE: None of yer…

ROBBIE: In an 'ome.

BOBBO: 'Ow come?

HORSE: Mind yer…

ROBBIE: She's not well. Costin us an all, every penny 'e gets from 'is pension goes towards keepin 'er there. So 'e's 'ad to come 'ere 'cos 'e can't do fuckin nish to look after 'imself.

BOBBO: Is she private?

HORSE: That's right private, as in none of yer business.

BOBBO: Which one's she in?

ROBBIE: The one on…

HORSE: (*Zips his mouth.*) Zip it.

ROBBIE: I'll zip somethin in a minute.

HORSE: I don't want 'im to know.

ROBBIE: Why what 'arm can it do?

HORSE: Plenty, now just leave it there will yer?

ROBBIE: The 'eat's melted 'is brain.

BOBBO: 'S'arlight 'e's just like me own Da in'e.

ROBBIE: Pair of tight arses.

BOBBO: Remember 'ow they 'ad us turnin up at school.

ROBBIE: Like beggars.

BOBBO: Big fuck off 'oles in our shoes.

ROBBIE: Or yer sole 'angin off.

BOBBO: If it rained yer socks would get all wet and start hangin out of the holes in the front, wouldn't they?. They'd keep comin out until they was dead long; like big fuck off tongues, until they'd be slappin up at yer like that. (*Demonstrates.*) They'd be comin up and slappin yer in the face as yer walked 'ome from school.

ROBBIE: I 'ad the same pair of shorts from the age of nine right up till I was 14. I remember comin back from a cross country run and walkin down the corridor to the changing rooms and the bell 'ad just gone fer dinner or 'ome time or something, so's all kids from other classes an that was walking up the corridor and for some reason I looked down, and me shorts were so short that me knob was poking out the fuckin bottom. I near fuckin died, I dived into them changing rooms like a fuckin whippet and then 'ad to go 'ome and blag 'is 'ead fer new ones. Next fuckin salute he comes 'ome and he's got me two new pairs; fuckin bright purple! Everyone was laughin at me behind me back. And 'e wonders why I never got a bird at school.

HORSE looks hurt.

BOBBO: Mad wan'it?

ROBBIE: We got into some fights over all that shit.

BOBBO: Learned to respect us though didn't they?

ROBBIE looks down at his feet and they are uneasily quiet for a few moments.

Right, give us the records then and I'll get me gone.

ROBBIE: They're in that case.

BOBBO: Sound.

ROBBIE: Make sure yer get top dollar Bobbo.

BOBBO: I'll sort it.

ROBBIE: Right.

BOBBO gets up and picks up the suitcase.

HORSE: What's with the big case?

ROBBIE: That's some rare Vinyl in there, needs protectin.

HORSE: What Vinyl?

ROBBIE: Nothin, drink yer can.

HORSE: That's not Wayne's records in there is it?

ROBBIE: My records.

HORSE: Since when are they yours? You don't even like music. Yer didn't even like 'er music.

ROBBIE: I did like 'er music.

HORSE: Yer didn't! Yer didn't understand 'er.

ROBBIE: Course I did.

HORSE: Not like me and Wayne.

ROBBIE: You think yer fuckin knew Tina, eh Dad? You don't know the fuckin 'alf of it mate.

BOBBO is lapping this up.

HORSE: You don't know what yer talking about.

ROBBIE: What is it with you an 'er anyway?

HORSE: What?

ROBBIE: Did yer fuckin fancy 'er.

HORSE: Don't be disgustin.

ROBBIE: Is that it? Did yer fancy yer chances with T?

HORSE: You take that back.

ROBBIE: Think she might 'ave bin too stoned to notice it was the father and not the son.

HORSE: Yer sick.

ROBBIE: What is it then?

HORSE: (*Pause.*) She was special. She deserved better than you.

Pause.

BOBBO: James is waitin.

HORSE stands up.

HORSE: They're 'is records!

ROBBIE: It's only a few.

HORSE: They're not goin anywhere.

ROBBIE: Says who?

HORSE: Says me.

HORSE makes a grab for the suitcase but ROBBIE gets in the way.

ROBBIE: Sit down.

HORSE: No.

ROBBIE: Sit down!

HORSE body automatically shifts into a boxer stance. There is something saddening and pathetic about it.

HORSE: Give 'em 'ere!

ROBBIE pushes HORSE hard and he falls backwards on to the sofa.

ROBBIE: I SAID SIT DOWN!

HORSE is shocked.

BOBBO: Yer couldn't've done that to 'im once.

ROBBIE: (*To BOBBO.*) Are you still 'ere?

BOBBO: Alright keep yer 'ead on yer neck. Meet us in the JB in about two hours.

ROBBIE: This is the last lot Bobbo.

BOBBO: But what about…

ROBBIE: I'm gonna 'ave to find some other way of makin money.

BOBBO: If yer say so.

ROBBIE: Oh I say so.

BOBBO walks out through the living room door and we hear him leave the flat through the front door.

ROBBIE looks down at his father, who looks back at him as though he were a stranger.

ROBBIE: Maybe I wasn't good enough fer T. But I'll yell yer somethin, your not good enough fer Mam, never was and never will be.

Music – 'You Never Give Me Your Money' by the Beatles.

HORSE starts to weep into his hands, ROBBIE goes to touch him but can't and instead leaves the room and out through the front door.

Fade to blackout.

Scene 3: The Lizard

The living room, the next day, teatime. ROBBIE and HORSE are sitting on separate couches, watching the TV. ROBBIE is counting out money on the table. Music fades.

ROBBIE: I feel like I've found the other end of the rainbow 'ere.

HORSE: (*Indicates something on the TV screen.*) Kip of that.

ROBBIE: (*Sarcastic.*) New Deal.

HORSE: She never gets 'er 'air quite right does she?

ROBBIE: Who?

HORSE: Carol Vorderman.

ROBBIE: Yer make yer own deals in life.

HORSE: Clever tart though.

ROBBIE: I mean what was I doin?

HORSE: Good legs.

ROBBIE: I'll tell yer what an all…

HORSE: She's a Lizard though.

ROBBIE: …I'm gonna give this place a lick of paint.

HORSE: Anyone that successful 'as to be a Lizard. Blair, Bush, Jackson, Copperfield, Vorderman.

ROBBIE gets up and goes to the window and looks out.

She probably blew the space shuttle up.

ROBBIE: Redecorate.

HORSE: Both times.

ROBBIE: Brighten things up around 'ere is what I'm gonna do.

HORSE: Nothin we can do about it though, they're in charge.

ROBBIE: Get sorted.

HORSE: New recruits every day.

ROBBIE: Fresh start an that.

HORSE: Trevor McDonut an all them at ITN. BBC team'll be next.

ROBBIE: Wayne in 'is room?

HORSE: What?

ROBBIE: Where's Wayne?

HORSE: Out.

ROBBIE: Again? What's got into 'im?

HORSE: I made 'im wear baby oil to keep 'im from burnin in that sun though.

ROBBIE: Nice one. 'Ow longs 'e bin?

ROBBIE goes into the kitchen.

HORSE: Hours.

ROBBIE gets a couple of cans from the fridge.

ROBBIE: Is 'e tryin to score a weed after all that I got 'im yesterday?

HORSE: What?

ROBBIE: Nothin.

ROBBIE re-enters the living room and passes a can to HORSE.

HORSE: Ta.

ROBBIE: D'yer want some of this Dad. (*Indicates money.*)

HORSE: You know 'ow I feel about that.

ROBBIE: I've put an end to it.

HORSE: And now what? Cos that won't last.

ROBBIE: I'll think of somethin.

Pause.

WAYNE bursts into the flat through the front door, and heads for the living room. Both men jump. He has a plastic bag full of take-out food and is excited.

WAYNE: Never fear Wayne is 'ere.

ROBBIE goes into the hall and hides the bag behind the bin bags near the front door.

HORSE: Somethin smells nice.

ROBBIE enters the living room.

ROBBIE: I didn't 'ear the lift.

WAYNE: I ran up.

ROBBIE: Ran up?

WAYNE: All the way.

HORSE: In this 'eat?

WAYNE: Don't wanna let this lot get cold do I.

HORSE: Yer must be mad, lad.

WAYNE: I'm alright.

HORSE: Is that Take Away?

WAYNE: I 'ope yers are 'ungry.

ROBBIE: Why what 'ave yer got there?

WAYNE: Fer you Dad, I've got Chicken Korma, rice and a garlic Naan.

WAYNE takes some wrapped up cartons from the bag and hands it to ROBBIE. He then pulls out some more food.

And for me I've got, Chicken Buna, rice and a plain naan, and fer you Grandad, I've got a boiled egg.

WAYNE produces a pickled egg.

HORSE: Is that it?

WAYNE: Wait fer it. And yer auld favourite. Spanish omelette, peas and fish scraps.

WAYNE takes out his Granddad's food and passes it him.

HORSE: Ta la.

ROBBIE: Who 'ave you mugged?

WAYNE: The general public.

ROBBIE: Who?

WAYNE: Only I didn't mug 'em, I hypnotised 'em.

ROBBIE: You've lost the plot you.

WAYNE pulls a bag full of coins from his pocket, and throws it on the table.

ROBBIE: 'Ow much is there?

WAYNE: Just under thirty.

ROBBIE: 'Ave yer done the launderette?

WAYNE: I earned it.

ROBBIE: Earned it, 'ow?

WAYNE: 'Ow d'yer think?

ROBBIE: Yer 'aven't sold yer arse 'ave yer Wayne?

WAYNE: Stop smokin crack Dad.

HORSE: 'Ow did yer earn it kid?

WAYNE: Buskin.

HORSE: Buskin?

ROBBIE: Buskin?

WAYNE: Buskin.

ROBBIE: Where?

WAYNE: In town.

ROBBIE: You earned all that from singin songs in town?

WAYNE: My songs.

ROBBIE: Yeah?

WAYNE: People loved me Dad, I couldn't believe it meself.
I could only whisper 'em at first and then I just went fer
it and now I know.

ROBBIE: I can't believe it.

HORSE: What d'yer now know Wayne?

WAYNE: I'm gonna make it.

HORSE: It's just buskin lad, people might 'ave felt sorry fer
yer.

WAYNE: No they didn't.

ROBBIE: People gave yer this?

WAYNE: Things are gonna change round 'ere Dad, you'll
see.

WAYNE goes into the kitchen and gets out some plates.

Where's all the forks?

ROBBIE: (*Looking at the bag of money in his hands in disbelief.*)
'Ow's 'e done that?

*WAYNE comes back in with three knives and hands two of
them to HORSE and ROBBIE. They start to eat, using the
knifes as forks.*

WAYNE: A record producer's interested in me an all. Told
me to go and see 'im sometime.

ROBBIE: Yeah?

WAYNE: Oh yeah.

HORSE: Doesn't mean a thing.

WAYNE: Thanks Grandad, but it means shit loads.

HORSE: Don't go there kid.

WAYNE: Why not?

HORSE: Look what 'appened to yer Mother yer stupid little prick!

WAYNE: What's that gotta do with me?

HORSE: Tell 'im Robbie.

ROBBIE: It won't last 'e's a pot 'ead.

WAYNE: I'm goin again tomorrow.

HORSE: Yer bloody not!

WAYNE: I bloody am!

HORSE: But Wayne yer know where it all leads. Robbie will yer knock...

WAYNE: Yer said it yerself Grandad, I'm not 'er. I'm not gonna lose it if I fail at this, and I'm not gonna fail.

HORSE: Yer don't know what yer gettin yerself into.

WAYNE: I do though.

HORSE: No yer fuckin don't Wayne. These people who make yer promises they're...

WAYNE: What? Fuckin Lizards? (*Pause.*) Yer just a stupid auld man Grandad who's read to many books about shite. Don't yer see what I'm tryin to do 'ere? Dad might 'ave won a few bets but that won't last. I've gone out and earned money.

ROBBIE: Can't we just eat this?

WAYNE: I'm gonna provide fer us. Me!

HORSE: You? You couldn't provide a hole fer a sailor.

WAYNE: Shut up.

HORSE: Don't you disrespect me.

ROBBIE: Let's just enjoy this eh?

HORSE: Look at yer, I could make two of yer out of me leg and yer think yer gonna provide fer us.

ROBBIE: I'm providin fer us.

HORSE: You're not good enough Wayne, I want yer to take the strings off that guitar and leave it be.

WAYNE: You didn't see me I was…

HORSE: A skinny little poor kid who everyone felt sorry fer and so they tossed 'im some spare change what was weighin them down anyway. (*TO ROBBIE.*) Yer shouldn't 'ave bought 'im strings.

ROBBIE: I didn't know 'e'd start fuckin buskin.

HORSE: I want yer to throw that guitar away Wayne.

WAYNE: 'Ow can yer sit there and tell me not to follow me dream when yer've abandoned yer wife.

HORSE: What did you say?

ROBBIE: Wayne!

WAYNE: After all them years together with yer books and cartoons and she gets a bit fuckin ill and yer just stick 'er in an 'ome and leave 'er to it.

ROBBIE: Are you looking fer a slap.

HORSE: You don't know what yer talkin about.

WAYNE: Don't I? I think I do. I'm talkin about a selfish auld man who's left his wife to sit in 'er own shit, because she can't boil yer a fuckin egg no more!

HORSE: That's not true!

ROBBIE: Leave it.

WAYNE: I've been to see 'er. I've seen Nan and I've seen the nurses who look after 'er. We 'ad a chat, oh yeah, and d'yer know what? He hasn't been to see 'er since he fuckin stuck 'er there, not once. And I'll tell yer something else an all, she 'asn't got Alzheimers and she isn't sick. She's upset, that's what she is, really upset an sad. I couldn't get 'er to tell me why, but 'e knows; that's what she said that 'e knows.

ROBBIE: She's not sick?

WAYNE: No.

ROBBIE: What's 'appened then.

HORSE: I can't...

ROBBIE: What the fuck's 'appened?

HORSE: Leave me...

ROBBIE: I mean the pair of yer were never apart, all those fuckin years, I've never known anything like it. Yers did everythin together, everythin.

HORSE: I know I...

ROBBIE: Did you 'it 'er? Is that it? Did yers 'ave a tiff and you 'it 'er.

HORSE: No...

ROBBIE: Yer couldn't 'it a man anymore, so yer 'it me Mam is that it? Was yer ashamed of the fact that the last time yer stood in a ring and faced a man yer fuckin pissed yerself instead, in front of me, in front of 'er. So you took it out on me Mam all these years later because every time yer looked at 'er yer felt smaller and smaller?

HORSE: NO!

ROBBIE: DID YOU HIT MY MUM!

HORSE: NO!

ROBBIE: WHAT DID YER FUCKIN DO?

HORSE: NOTHIN! THAT'S JUST IT, I DIDN'T DO NOTHIN!!! (*Beat.*) And she had to pay.

ROBBIE: I don't understand.

HORSE: (*Sobbing now.*) I'm a coward.

ROBBIE: What's 'appened?

HORSE: I can't tell yer.

ROBBIE: You can.

HORSE: Poor Alice.

ROBBIE: Tell me.

HORSE: I couldn't 'elp...

ROBBIE: Somethin 'appened.

HORSE: Please.

ROBBIE grabs his Father's arm.

ROBBIE: Why 'ave yer left 'er?

HORSE: She 'ates me.

ROBBIE: Mam?

WAYNE: Not Nan.

HORSE's tears are falling harder now and they physically hurt him.

HORSE: She can't... She can't bear to look at me.

WAYNE: What makes yer think that, Grandad?

HORSE: Because I didn't stop 'im.

WAYNE: Who?

ROBBIE: What are yer tryin to say 'ere Dad?

HORSE: We was...was...it was night an...oh God...forgot... I forgot to lock...an we was...was in bed...reading...both of us...an 'e got in... I couldn't... I wanted to but I... I mean I used to be... I used to...couldn't move see... I tried to...honest I tried to but... I... I wouldn't...

WAYNE: What's he sayin Dad?

ROBBIE: Someone broke into the house Dad?

HORSE: Oh God...stood there...stood...

ROBBIE: Did 'e 'it yer?

HORSE: Alice 'e...please don't...don't make 'er... 'e shouldn't of made 'er do that...

ROBBIE: What are yer sayin?

HORSE: I couldn't...move...

ROBBIE: What 'appened?

HORSE: 'E...she...she wet the...but even...even then 'e still...

ROBBIE: WHAT HAPPENED!

HORSE: 'E touched... 'e made 'er...do, 'e...

ROBBIE: Touched 'er?

HORSE: 'E did... 'e made...made Alice... he...and she... she 'ad to do it...

WAYNE: Oh God.

HORSE: I was to... I tried to...but I couldn't yer see... couldn't move and now she...she...

ROBBIE: Are you sayin someone...someone raped Mam?

HORSE is lost to his tears.

WAYNE: No.

ROBBIE: Someone broke in an raped me Mam?

HORSE nods his head.

WAYNE: Me Nan.

ROBBIE: (*Painful confusion.*) But she's an auld woman!

HORSE: I couldn't...me nerves... I was... I...

ROBBIE grabs hold of HORSE around the collar.

ROBBIE: Why didn't yer stop him?

WAYNE tries to pull his Dad off his Granddad.

WAYNE: Get off him.

ROBBIE: Yer supposed to be a man.

WAYNE: You'll hurt him.

ROBBIE: You was a fuckin boxer fer Christ sake!

WAYNE: Get off 'im Dad.

ROBBIE: Why didn't yer kill 'im.

WAYNE: E's old Dad.

ROBBIE: Tell me yer fuckin makin this up.

WAYNE: Dad!

ROBBIE: Yer should of fuckin done something. 'Ow could yer just lie there and let 'im do that to…and then yer just stuck 'er in an 'ome like she was used goods is that it?

WAYNE: Let go of 'im.

ROBBIE: Too dirty fer yer to look at is she?

HORSE: She won't look at me. She thinks I'm a coward.

ROBBIE slaps HORSE on the side of the head and face. It is not a hard blow but it is by know means a soft blow either.

ROBBIE: You're not a coward are yer Dad?

He slaps him again.

ROBBIE: Come on get up.

WAYNE: Don't Dad.

ROBBIE: Get up and do something about it.

Another slap.

What fuckin 'appened to you 'ey? (*Pause.*) I saw yer knock fellahs twice yer size out the ring. I mean what the fuck's up with yer Dad… me Ma… I mean yer can't tell me…she's… Who is he? Dad, I wanna know who this filthy fuckin bastard was.

HORSE: I can't…

ROBBIE: I wanna know who this sick twat is, so's I can fuckin go and get him.

WAYNE: Not now Dad.

ROBBIE: Who is 'e?

HORSE: I don't…don't… I've never seen 'im… 'ad a mask on.

ROBBIE: Yer must know, yer must 'ave some sort of fuckin idea.

HORSE: If I'd bin younger…

ROBBIE: What colour was 'is eyes?

HORSE: Lizard…

ROBBIE: Don't push me Dad.

HORSE: Lizard eyes.

ROBBIE: Don't give me that shit now. Yer pathetic enough without rollin in that shit now.

HORSE: I was scared I…

WAYNE: Leave 'im.

ROBBIE: (*Utter despair.*) Me Mam…

HORSE: Oh God I'm so sorry…

ROBBIE: Come on Dad I need somethin to grab onto 'ere. I can't do this on me own, I need yer 'elp; Mam needs yer 'elp. Just tell me what 'e was like and I'll fuckin tear 'im apart.

WAYNE: Dad…

ROBBIE: I told you to button it.

HORSE: I couldn't move.

ROBBIE: I'll bring 'im back 'ere; you'd like that wouldn't yer? Bring 'im back 'ere and yer can kill 'im.

HORSE: No…

ROBBIE: Bring 'im back 'ere and yer can go to town on the sick fucker.

HORSE: I don't want 'im ere; I don't want 'im near me.

ROBBIE: Who? Who is 'e?

HORSE: I don't know!

ROBBIE: You do!

HORSE: I don't!

ROBBIE: Yer must!

HORSE: I don't!

ROBBIE: Yer must, yer must, yer 'ave to or I can't fuckin find 'im.

HORSE: I don't know.

ROBBIE: Think.

HORSE: I am thinkin, I'm thinkin so 'ard it 'urts.

ROBBIE: Please Dad!

WAYNE: What about Nan?

ROBBIE: Was it Bobbo? Is that why yer afraid of 'im. Was it 'im?

HORSE: No.

ROBBIE: TELL ME!

HORSE: I'm confused…

WAYNE: SHUT UP! BOTH OF YERS JUST SHUT UP!

Pause.

It's not about you Dad and it's not about 'im, it's about Nan. She's been raped; I can't think of a worse thing that can 'appen to a woman and she's just been left all on 'er own to deal with it.

ROBBIE bursts into tears.

She needs you now more than ever Grandad. Why aren't you there comforting 'er?

HORSE: She hates me, she can't bear to look at me she's that disgusted with me.

WAYNE: But what if she can't bear to look at yer because she's ashamed of 'erself?

HORSE: God forgive me.

WAYNE: Maybe she thinks that you see 'er differently now; that yer wouldn't want 'er after what's 'appened.

HORSE: She's my baby…

WAYNE: Then hold her, take 'er in yer arms and…just do somethin.

HORSE: She doesn't want me.

WAYNE: I think she does. But 'er pride's been shattered, I think she thinks that you've abandoned 'er because she's…been made dirty.

HORSE: No, I'd never, I love 'er more than God.

WAYNE: Then go to 'er. March right in there and pick 'er up, and smell 'er 'air and ask why it smells so good, when she doesn't use spray, and tell 'er that you love 'er more than ever. (*Pause.*) Take 'er 'ome Grandad.

HORSE slowly stands; he tries to straighten his crumpled clothes. WAYNE goes over to his bags and picks one up and offers it HORSE.

I got yer some new clobber.

HORSE takes the bag.

I'm sorry it all came out the way it did. I was gonna talk to you about it when Dad wasn't 'ere but you kept pushin me. I never knew what 'ad 'appened. So I'm sorry.

HORSE undresses and takes the clothes from the bag; he looks them over and then dresses himself in them. WAYNE helps.

ROBBIE watches with a terrible rage brewing inside him. HORSE stops at it and turns and looks at ROBBIE .

HORSE: Robbie?

HORSE goes over to his son and puts a hand on his shoulder. ROBBIE pushes it away and spits in his father's face. They stare at each other for a moment and then ROBBIE out the front door, taking his terrible purpose with him.

Yer better go after yer Dad, 'e might do somethin he regrets.

WAYNE: Yeah I will.

HORSE: Thanks kid.

WAYNE goes after his Dad.

Music - 'Treat her Gently (Lonely old People)' by Wings

HORSE goes over to the couch against the back wall and kneels down.

He puts his hand underneath it and recovers the bag with the books in and stands up again. He takes the books out of the bag and looks at them. He puts them back into the bag and walks toward the door.

Fade to blackout.

Scene 4: Lizard Trail

Three hours have passed; the flat is empty. Music fades. After a moment or two there is a knock at the front door, then another, followed by a shout through the letterbox.

BOBBO: (*Through letterbox.*) Robbie. (*Pause.*) Robbie, you in? (*Pause.*) Robbie.

There is a fumbling at the door and then BOBBO enters the flat. He stands for a moment in the hall.

Anyone in? (*Pause.*) No?

BOBBO enters the living room has a quick look around, goes over to the window and looks out. He scans the streets below. Satisfied that no one is approaching he darts back into the hall and grabs one of the bin bags from the behind the front door and takes it out to the flat and jams the lift doors open with it. He re-enters the flat and enters WAYNE's room. He looks up at the picture of Tina on the wall.

Now then gorgeous, looks like it's just me an you.

BOBBO turns to the cupboard under the record player and kneels down before it. He opens the cupboards and runs his fingers over the spines of the records. He takes out the copy of 'Rubber Soul', and then 'Revolver' and 'Sgt Peppers Lonely Hearts Club Band'. He quickly takes a plastic bag out of his pocket and unfolds it, and then places the records in the bag. He stands up and turns to leave, he looks again at the picture of Tina and stops.

What's up love? Feel a bit left out. Soon sort that Queen.

BOBBO turns back to the cupboard and scans the spines once more.

There you are.

He pulls out Tina's record and is about to add it to the bag, when ROBBIE suddenly appears at the door. He is panting, from running up the stairs, his hands are dirty, and the knuckles on each are covered in dried blood, there is also a cut on his forehead. BOBBO becomes aware of him and turns round hiding the bag behind his back.

ROBBIE: (*Ice cold.*) Hello.

BOBBO: I… er… I've bin looking fer you.

ROBBIE: Looks like yer found me.

BOBBO: What's appened?

ROBBIE: You tell me.

BOBBO: Ave yer ad a fight?

ROBBIE: Sort of.

BOBBO: Who with?

ROBBIE: Brick wall.

BOBBO: You alright?

ROBBIE: I've bin looking fer you see?

BOBBO: Lookin fer me?

ROBBIE: You've bin looking fer me and I've bin looking fer you.

BOBBO: Yeah?

ROBBIE: Only thing is I couldn't find yer and I got a bit frustrated with that an so I took it out on a wall.

BOBBO: Jesus Robbie, yer a mess.

ROBBIE: Should see the wall.

BOBBO: What's goin on mate?

ROBBIE: What ave yer got behind yer back, mate?

BOBBO: Nothin.

ROBBIE: Show me.

BOBBO: Robbie I can explain...

ROBBIE: Show me!

BOBBO: I'm... Me bird she...

ROBBIE: (*Finger on lip.*) Shhh. (*Pause.*) Now do as yer told.

BOBBO brings the bag of records and Tina's still visible record from behind his back.

BOBBO: Listen...

ROBBIE: Is that Tina's record?

BOBBO: I was just looking at it; I wasn't goin to take it.

ROBBIE: Not like the ones in the bag yer mean?

BOBBO: No… I mean what would I want it fer? It's not like it's… (*Realises what he is about to say and stops.*)

ROBBIE: Not like it's what?

BOBBO: Yer know.

ROBBIE: No.

BOBBO: Worth anythin.

ROBBIE: (*Almost a whisper.*) Come ere.

BOBBO: What

ROBBIE: (*A little louder.*) Come ere.

BOBBO: What are yer goin to do.

ROBBIE: COME HERE!

BOBBO slowly inches towards ROBBIE, holding Tina's record between them as though it might protect him. When he is close he stops, he has an idea.

BOBBO: Try anything and I'll fuckin snap it.

BOBBO drops the bag and holds the record out as though to snap it. They stare at each other long and hard but something in ROBBIE's eyes breaks BOBBO's resolve to carry out his threat. Instead he slowly puts it on WAYNE's bed.

ROBBIE: Now come ere.

BOBBO edges closer.

BOBBO: Don't…

ROBBIE put his hands on BOBBO's shoulders.

ROBBIE: Did yer like goin into auld people's 'omes.

BOBBO: (*Utterly confused.*) What?

ROBBIE: Answer the fucking question.

BOBBO: I didn't think about it, it was easy money.

ROBBIE: Did yer get off on it though?

BOBBO: Off on what?

ROBBIE: Bein in their 'ouse and 'avin all that power over 'em. Bet yer got off on that big fuckin time eh? Goin through their draws whilst they're makin yer a cup of tea.

BOBBO: I was on the gear, I was off me 'ead.

ROBBIE: Did any of 'em ever catch yer at it like, forgot 'ow many sugars yer'd said yer'd 'ad and come back to ask yer and found yer rifflin through their fuckin knickers draw?

BOBBO: What's all this about?

ROBBIE: Did thee or didn't thee?

BOBBO: I got 'it by a poker once.

ROBBIE: A poker?

BOBBO: On the back of the 'ead.

ROBBIE: Whilst yer was in 'er draws?

BOBBO: Nearly knocked me out.

ROBBIE: What did yer do?

BOBBO: The only thing I could do.

ROBBIE: What was that?

BOBBO: I pushed 'er over and got out quick.

ROBBIE: Just pushed 'er over?

BOBBO: Yeah.

ROBBIE: Some auld bird with a beard and no teeth caves yer 'ead in from behind and yer just pushed 'er over and got off quick.

BOBBO: What else am I gonna do?

me over. The round started, he was good, fast, graceful even, he got a few digs in, scored some points and then it came, an openin and took it like I'd never took anything before, I put everythin into that one punch, me heart, me soul, everythin. If I'd missed I'd 'ave been finished, to tired to go on, but I didn't miss, I caught him clean in the right temple, I heard 'is skull crunch and felt 'is brain turn to mush. He went down like a bag of water, blood comin out of 'is ears and nose. And before he hit the deck, I saw the lights go out in 'is eyes. They never came back on, 'e never stood up again; 'is mother 'ad to spoon-feed 'im. It broke me kid, broke what's inside. Everyone thought I was some sort of legend, but I was crucified fer what I'd done, I wanted to shatter 'im completely an I did. I lost it then, broke down, lost me bottle, became afraid of these.

HORSE holds his hands before him and studies them, they no longer shake.

The next fight you were at, yer begged yer Mam to bring yer, she didn't wanna go, but you screamed until she did. I couldn't face it, everythin just fell out of me. I ran away, I've bin runnin ever since, until now that is.

ROBBIE: 'Ow did yer keep that from us?

HORSE: It was an illegal match; stories were made up an people kept stum about it. Alice couldn't speak about it; I think she came close to leavin me then. If I adn't ave become so ill, I think she would 'ave,

ROBBIE: I didn't know.

HORSE: So when... when... 'e... came in the bedroom, I just froze, I was paralysed.

ROBBIE: What's changed?

HORSE: Alice.

ROBBIE: Mam?

HORSE: She's wiped the slate clean; wants a fresh start.

ROBBIE: 'Ow is she?

HORSE: She's getting better Son, it's gonna be a long 'ard road fer 'er, fer both of us, but we're gonna make it work, she wants me to get the 'ouse ready.

Pause.

ROBBIE: I don't know what to do.

HORSE: Wayne's got talent, real talent.

ROBBIE: So did she and look where that got 'er.

HORSE: So what, yer hold him back from his dream in case he becomes 'is mother?

ROBBIE: I can't go through all that again, watchin it slowly destroy 'im.

HORSE: But it could be the makin of 'im.

ROBBIE: What chance as 'e got?

HORSE: You've 'eard 'is songs, we both 'ave, I mean we try and pretend we 'aven't, turn the telly up or whatever, but we've 'eard 'im in that pit of 'is. They're beautiful, they need to see the light.

ROBBIE: 'E's buskin isn't 'e?

HORSE: Yeah, but that's not enough.

ROBBIE: It should 'ave bin me who died, not 'er.

HORSE: (*Strokes ROBBIE's head.*) No, no, no. She took 'er own life, don't let 'er memory control yours.

ROBBIE starts to cry.

HORSE comforts him for a moment.

I've gotta go now Robbie; sort the 'ouse out, get it fit fer a Queen.

HORSE leaves.

Music – 'Oh My Love' by John Lennon.

ROBBIE walks into the kitchen and runs the cold tap, he then puts his head under it for a few moment; he then comes back into the living room shaking the water from his head. He looks about him, he goes into the kitchen and he takes a bin bag from the drawer in there and comes back in. He then starts to clean up; putting rubbish into the bag. He grabs the bucket from the table, complete with bottle and takes it over to the window and pours the water out and throws the bottle. He then goes back into the kitchen with it and fills it with soapy water, he then re-enters the living room and starts to clean the walls with a cloth from the bucket. He stops for a moment and plucks the hair from the wall, that is Tina's. He looks at it, smells it and then takes it to the window and lets the breeze capture it and take it away. He then continues to scrub the walls.

Music fades.

Sound of front door being opened and WAYNE comes into the hall, he heads straight for the living room, where he sees ROBBIE washing the walls, his mouth falls open in shock.

WAYNE: What are yer doin to the walls?

ROBBIE: I'm washin 'em.

WAYNE: Don't.

ROBBIE: What?

WAYNE: Stop it.

ROBBIE: Wayne?

WAYNE: You'll wash Mum away.

ROBBIE: She wouldn't want us livin in a dirty 'ome?

WAYNE: What would you know what she wants?

ROBBIE: Because I fuckin know. It's took me long enough to realise it.

WAYNE: Realise what?

ROBBIE: That...

WAYNE notices that the hair is gone.

It's fer the best; trust me.

WAYNE: What 'ave yer done with it?

ROBBIE: Gave it back to 'er.

WAYNE: What's that supposed to mean?

ROBBIE: It's gone.

WAYNE: Why?

ROBBIE: I'm cleanin up.

WAYNE: Don't you wash any more of this room.

ROBBIE: Wayne listen...

WAYNE storms out and runs into his bedroom slamming the door shut behind him.

ROBBIE stands still for a moment and then continues to clean.

At the same time WAYNE paces around the room. He stops looks at the picture of Tina and then he fiddles around in his pocket until he produces a lighter. He takes the hat and puts it on and then lights the candles. WAYNE then sits on the corner of the bed for a moment and looks at the cupboard under the record player. He leans forward and opens the cupboard, something is different; there are gaps in the rows of records. WAYNE's hands flicker over the spines in frantic confirmation, before plucking them out in wads to see what is still there. WAYNE is horrified at his discoveries.

WAYNE: (*Anguish.*) What 'ave yer done?

ROBBIE stops and enters WAYNE's bedroom.

ROBBIE: Look...

WAYNE: What 'ave yer done with 'em?

ROBBIE: I've sold 'em.

WAYNE: Don't lie.

ROBBIE: There's still loads left.

WAYNE: Give us 'em back now.

ROBBIE: I didn't mean to take so many.

WAYNE: I'll find 'em if yer won't show us.

ROBBIE: Kept thinking another, yer won't notice a few more.

WAYNE: I'll close me eyes and yer can get 'em and put 'em back.

ROBBIE: They're gone.

WAYNE: Put them back.

ROBBIE: They're gone.

WAYNE: Why?

ROBBIE: I can't undo it.

WAYNE: You…

ROBBIE: I'm sorry, I thought it was the only way, I wasn't thinkin straight; I was looking fer a quick answer.

WAYNE: So you've sold 'em?

ROBBIE: Fer good money.

WAYNE is shaking with anger.

WAYNE: Fer good money?

ROBBIE: I don't mean it like that, I mean we wasn't ripped off.

WAYNE: Kept 'em in good condition fer a smack head, didn't she?

ROBBIE: You what?

WAYNE: Worth more in good knick are they Dad? How much fer this one?

WAYNE holds up a record.

'Beatles fer Sale', not their best album but it's an original and it's signed by the boys and what d'yer reckon Dad, get us a few weeks shoppin and a couple of take aways or what?

WAYNE takes the record out of its sleeve. He is boiling over now.

Maybe some beers an all.

WAYNE suddenly brings the record hard down on the record player, shattering it into pieces.

ROBBIE: What are yer doin?

WAYNE: Shit, there not worth as much when there damaged. Never mind plenty more where that came from eh Dad?

WAYNE picks up another record and takes it from the sleeve.

We've got a Frankie one 'ere, signed by Holly, we could get some weed fer it eh, or maybe we should wait until 'e dies of aids, it might be worth a bit more then.

WAYNE smashes it like the other.

ROBBIE: Stop it!

WAYNE: Won't get as much fer it now.

WAYNE takes more records and starts to smash them.

ROBBIE: Stop it!

WAYNE sees his mother's album on the bed. He picks it up.

WAYNE: What's up yer 'aven't flogged this one?

ROBBIE: I'd never…

WAYNE: Couldn't get a buyer fer it?

ROBBIE: Listen…

WAYNE: Surely yer could of got a few quid fer Mum.

WAYNE takes the vinyl from the sleeve.

But that was the problem wasn't it? No body ever did want to buy it.

ROBBIE: Don't...

WAYNE: It's worthless is that it? Not worth shit!

ROBBIE: Course it is.

WAYNE: Who to? You? Yer never could stand it.

ROBBIE: Listen to me a min...

WAYNE: LISTEN TO THIS!!!

WAYNE brings his mother's record down hard against the cupboard and smashes it. They look at the pieces on the floor and the shard in WAYNE's hand and then at each other. Wayne starts to sob.

Look what you made me do.

ROBBIE: I...

WAYNE: I've broke 'er. (*Pause.*) What am I gonna do?

ROBBIE: I don't know.

Pause.

WAYNE: Why couldn't it 'ave been you? (*Pause.*) You should of died instead.

ROBBIE: I've spent every day since wishing that I 'ad Wayne, cos that would 'ave been a lot easier fer me.

WAYNE: She was worth a million of you, yer nothin, nothin!

Pause.

ROBBIE: Sometimes someone shines so bright from within that the glare from them pushes the shadows right into the corners. But those shadows are still there Wayne, like tar, and that's where I've been, in the dark, stuck in those shadows. When people came here or saw us together,

they only really saw Tina, not me, it's like I didn't exist.
I did everythin for yer, right from a baby right up to
now. 'Ow many fellahs round 'ere would let their wife go
up and down the country chasin their dream in the back
of a van with a bunch of smackheads, whilst they stayed
at 'ome and looked after the kid, who kept crying fer 'er
to come 'ome all day and night. Knowin deep down that
it was all goin to be fer nothing anyway. She use to go
on about that record collection like it was some sort of
link to success, that she only 'ad to join 'erself to it with
'er record and the rest would follow, like it was the
missing cog that would set the Liverpool scene on fire
again. But it's all...all rusted up like some auld steam
train that's been left in a swamp. I remember them
telling us at school that Liverpool was a marsh before
anyone settled 'ere; that they 'ad to drain it. Yeah well,
they forgot to switch the thing off and it's been draining
away ever since and now it's a fuckin desert.

WAYNE: Mum could've changed that.

ROBBIE: No she couldn't, not with a needle 'angin out of
'er groin and neither will you unless yer take yer 'ead
out of that bucket and face things. (*Pause.*) It's just
another shadow to get lost in, we've all been doin it, Me
you and me Dad.

WAYNE: I've been out buskin 'aven't I? People like me
songs.

ROBBIE: It's not enough Wayne, you've got to do more
than that. 'Ow many buskers are on *Top of the Pops*?

WAYNE: What more can I do? Try me luck on *Pop Idol*?

ROBBIE: You can get serious, clear yer 'ead of weed and
use yer pain to write those songs that break peoples
hearts, the one that just 'it yer right 'ere. (*Slaps chest.*)

WAYNE: 'Ow can I when you and Grandad 'ave always put
me down.

ROBBIE: I don't think 'e'll ever doubt yer again, d'you? (*Pause.*) As fer me, I was just scared I was gonna end up in another shadow; yours.

Pause.

WAYNE: Why weren't we enough Dad?

ROBBIE: It's not our fault.

WAYNE: We must've done something wrong.

ROBBIE: What more could we 'ave done?

WAYNE: Why didn't yer support 'er?

ROBBIE: I did. I supported 'er by supportin you. I looked after you while she worked at 'er thing, an then when she broke down, I still 'ad me 'ands full tryin to keep yer from seein it. You was in bits too remember. I was scared you was gonna harm yerself.

WAYNE: I thought she was gonna be a star.

ROBBIE: She was, she still is, our star.

Pause.

WAYNE: I used to grab 'er face when she was…when she was…yer know…try and get 'er to look at me… I'd pull 'er round; try and look in 'er eyes, but…she wasn't there. (*Pause.*) She's 'ere now though, 'as been ever since… And now you're washin 'er away.

ROBBIE: Not from 'ere Wayne. (*Puts hand over heart.*) Or 'ere. (*puts hand over WAYNE's heart.*) I just think it's time to come out of the shadows, make our own light. (*Pause.*) I can't fix what's 'appened to me Mam, I can't even find the bastard who done it, but you fixed me Dad and 'e'll fix 'er in time and I'm so proud of yer fer what you've done. I think I'd go fuckin mad if it wasn't fer you. I thought that there was no 'ope in the world, that it 'ad died with T. But you, you go out there and yer fuckin do yer thing, with no encouragement from anyone, the opposite in fact, and I don't know if you've got a flyin fuck of a chance of makin it proper, but yer goin fer it and goin fer it the 'ard way and that's sparked something in me.

WAYNE: What?

ROBBIE: It's a fresh start. I'm gonna change, I'm gonna go back the dole and get that job, any job. I promise yer Wayne. I'll do anything fer yer... yer me life.

Pause.

I 'aven't pissed all that money up the wall yer know.

WAYNE: So.

ROBBIE: So, why don't yer buy a recordin desk with it?

WAYNE: What?

ROBBIE: Yer can record yer own album in yer bedroom like that Moby and cut out the middleman.

WAYNE: I don't know.

ROBBIE: It makes sense.

WAYNE: Yeah.

ROBBIE: Yeah.

WAYNE: I could do with a new guitar an all.

ROBBIE: Electric?

WAYNE: Oh yes. I'll need a keyboard as well.

ROBBIE: Now yer takin the piss.

WAYNE: And a drum machine.

WAYNE gives a small chuckle and ROBBIE follows suit.

ROBBIE: There should be just about enough.

WAYNE: Thanks.

ROBBIE: They was your records.

WAYNE: Our records. (*Pause.*) So what was we doin again?

ROBBIE: What d'yer mean, we was…

WAYNE: Oh I know.

Music – 'Oh My Love' by John Lennon (Reprised).

WAYNE takes the hat off and puts it in the cupboard and closes the door. He then blows out the candles and pulls them from the shelf.

Both men continue to clean the walls.

Lights fade to blackout.

The End.